CONQUERING THE LEVIATHAN SPIRIT

David S. Philemon

Royal Diadem Publishing Inc.

Conquering the Leviathan Spirit
978-1-966141-56-3

For permissions, additional information, or bulk order inquiries, please contact the author.

Write:
Royal Diadem Publishing Inc.
4836 W. 13th Street, Cicero, IL 60804
1 (312) 970-0183

Unless otherwise indicated, all Scripture quotations in this volume are taken from the King James Version (KJV) and the New King James Version (NKJV) of the Holy Bible.

Dedication

To the Almighty God, my Rock, Refuge, and Source of all wisdom and strength. Thank You for Your unwavering love, grace, and the purpose You've placed within me. May this book bring glory to Your name and draw others closer to You.

And to my beloved spiritual parents, Dr. Paul and Dr. Mrs. Becky Paul Enenche, who have faithfully nurtured and guided me in this journey. Your example of unwavering devotion, godly counsel, and compassionate care has been a beacon of light and strength in my life. Thank you for standing as pillars of faith and for your steadfast commitment to the Kingdom.

ACKNOWLEDGMENTS

This book would not have been possible without the unwavering support, dedication, and talent of an extraordinary team. My deepest gratitude goes to each of you for your contributions, insights, and encouragement throughout this journey.

First and foremost, thank you to Rev. Mimi Philemon my dear wife, Rev. Shina Gentry, and and my assistant pastor Rev. Bright Amudoaghan for your incredible effort, encouragement, and belief in this project. Your support has been instrumental in bringing this vision to life.

To the dedicated leaders of Royal Diadem Publishing, Ide Imogie and Kishawna Bailey, I am immensely grateful for your belief in this project from the very beginning and for investing your time and energy into its development. Your creativity, dedication, and expertise have been the backbone of this endeavor.

I am especially grateful to the Royal Diadem Publishing team— Beulah Orogun, Emmanuella Ben-Eboh, Doyinsade Awodele, Kim Matthews, and Shante Gill, for your meticulous attention to detail, refining every page and ensuring that each word reflects our vision.

A heartfelt thank you to my family, friends, and colleagues whose unwavering support and belief in this project gave me the courage and strength to see it through.

Finally, thank you to all the readers and supporters who make this work meaningful. I am humbled and honored to share this journey with each of you.

With all my gratitude,
David Philemon

CONTENTS

INTRODUCTION

Understanding The Leviathan Spirit

L eviathan is a powerful sea creature that is both mysterious and terrifying. It's mentioned in several places in Scripture, especially in the book of Job, where it's depicted as a fierce, untamable force of nature. But beyond its physical description, the Leviathan is often seen as a symbol of spiritual opposition—a spirit that works against God's people, bringing confusion, pride, and division. This book, "Defeating the Leviathan Spirit," is about understanding how this spirit operates today. While we may not see a literal sea monster like Leviathan, the spiritual impact of this force can still be felt in our personal lives, relationships, and even churches and communities. This book aims to help you recognize how the Leviathan spirit works, how it affects people, and, most importantly, how to overcome it through God's power. To begin, we need to understand what the Leviathan spirit represents. In the Bible, the Leviathan is more than just a sea creature. It symbolizes pride, chaos, and opposition to God's order. In Job 41, Leviathan is described as a creature that human strength cannot easily control or defeat. This picture of a robust and stubborn force can be seen as a metaphor for the spiritual battle many people face today. The Leviathan spirit is often connected with pride and self-exaltation. It tries to keep people focused on themselves rather than on God. It stirs up confusion and conflict, making people feel divided and distant from others. In churches and communities, this spirit can create strife, misunderstandings, and broken relationships, all rooted in pride and a lack of humility. The Bible tells us that God wants us to live in peace and unity with one another. In Ephesians 4:3, we are encouraged to "make every effort to keep the unity of the Spirit through the bond of peace." However, the Leviathan spirit works against this. It tries to destroy unity by causing division and conflict. For example, have you ever been in a situation where something small turns into a big argument, and no one seems willing to listen or understand each other? This is one way the Leviathan spirit operates—it takes minor issues and blows them out of proportion, making people feel defensive, misunderstood, or even superior to others. The result is a communication breakdown, and relationships suffer. God wants us to be free from pride and the chains of the Leviathan spirit. James 4:6 reminds us, "God opposes the proud but gives grace to the humble." This means that pride, which is a crucial trait of the Leviathan spirit, is something that separates us from God's grace. When we allow pride and confusion to rule our lives, we miss out on the peace, joy, and love God desires. God has given us the tools to overcome the Leviathan spirit. Through prayer, humility, and reliance on God's power, we can break free from the chains of pride and division. This book teaches you how to use spiritual warfare to fight back against the Leviathan spirit. You will discover how to identify its tactics, guard your heart against its influence, and live in the freedom that God offers.

One key aspect of defeating the Leviathan spirit is to walk in humility. James 4:10 says, "Humble yourselves before the Lord, and He will lift you." When we humble ourselves, we allow God to work in our hearts, breaking the strongholds of pride and healing our relationships. Another important aspect is the power of prayer and spiritual discernment. Ephesians 6:12: "Our struggle is not against flesh and blood but against the rulers, against the authorities, against the powers of this dark world and the spiritual forces of evil in the heavenly realms." While we live in a physical world, there is a spiritual reality that we cannot see with our natural eyes. The Bible teaches us that we are in the midst of a spiritual battle involving forces of good and evil. Recognizing this battle is essential because it affects our daily lives, relationships, and walk with God. This chapter will explore spiritual warfare, its necessity, and how believers can engage in it effectively. Spiritual warfare is a battle between God's kingdom and the forces of darkness. The enemy, Satan, seeks to destroy God's people and hinder their relationship with Him. The enemy uses various tactics to distract, deceive, and discourage believers. These tactics include temptation, confusion, fear, pride, and division. Spiritual warfare is standing firm against these attacks by relying on our power and authority in Christ. Spiritual warfare is essential because it impacts every area of our lives—from our thoughts and emotions to our relationships and decisions. Many challenges we face are physical or emotional and have a spiritual root. For instance, feelings of hopelessness, anxiety, or confusion may not always be caused by external circumstances but by spiritual forces trying to weigh us down. In relationships, conflicts often arise because of misunderstandings or personality clashes and because the enemy seeks to sow seeds of division and discord. The Leviathan spirit, for example, is a spirit of confusion and division, aiming to destroy unity in families, friendships, and churches. Recognizing this as part of spiritual warfare helps us understand that a more significant battle is at play, and we must fight it spiritually. The Bible repeatedly urges us to be watchful and prepared for spiritual battles. In 1 Peter 5:8, "Be alert and of sober mind. Your enemy, the devil, prowls around like a roaring lion looking for someone to devour." This means that spiritual warfare is not something we can ignore or take lightly. The enemy can take advantage of our weaknesses if we are not alert. Being prepared means equipping ourselves with spiritual armor. In Ephesians 6:13-18, Paul speaks about the armor of God, which includes the belt of truth, the breastplate of righteousness, the shield of faith, the helmet of salvation, the sword of the Spirit, and the readiness of the gospel of peace. This armor protects us from the enemy's attacks and helps us stand firm in our faith. Engaging in spiritual warfare strengthens our faith because it requires us to depend on God entirely. The battles we face are not won by our strength or wisdom but by relying on the power of God. Spiritual warfare is not about physical force but about using the spiritual weapons God has given us. As we trust God to fight our battles, our faith grows. We learn to rely more on His Word, pray more fervently, and seek His guidance in every situation. This dependence on God strengthens our relationship with Him and helps us stand firm in the face of opposition. Spiritual warfare is essential because it protects our spiritual growth. As Christians, we are called to grow in our relationship with God, becoming more like Christ in character and actions. However, the enemy will always try to hinder this growth by distracting us, tempting us to fall back into sin, or causing us to doubt God's goodness. We can protect our hearts and minds from these attacks through spiritual warfare. When we stand firm in the truth of God's Word and resist the enemy, we allow the Holy Spirit to guard our spiritual growth and lead us into a deeper relationship with God. In this book, we will explore the nature of the Leviathan spirit in depth. Each chapter will guide you through practical steps to recognize, confront, and defeat this spiritual force. We will also look at personal testimonies and biblical stories that illustrate how God delivers people from the grip of pride and division. As you read, you'll gain a deeper understanding of how the Leviathan spirit operates, but more importantly, you'll be equipped with the tools you need to overcome it. By the end of this journey, you will be empowered to live in the freedom and victory God has promised. Remember, the battle against the Leviathan spirit is not one you have to face alone. God is with you, and through His grace and power, you can defeat this spiritual enemy and live in peace and unity.

CHAPTER 1

THE NATURE OF THE LEVIATHAN SPIRIT

Leviathan is first mentioned in the Bible as a sea creature, often described as a serpent or dragon-like figure. In the book of Job, it is said to be a fierce, untamable creature (Job 41). One of the main characteristics of Leviathan is pride. It causes people to become proud and self-centered, thinking they are better than others or don't need help from God. Pride can blind us from seeing our own weaknesses and prevent us from being humble and loving toward others. Leviathan feeds off this pride, making it harder for people to admit their faults or ask for forgiveness, damaging relationships and separating people from God. Another tactic of the Leviathan spirit is to twist words. Just like a serpent twists and coils, Leviathan takes what people say and distorts it, causing misunderstandings. This can lead to conflicts and arguments, even when both parties have good intentions. Have you ever tried to explain yourself to someone, but they completely misunderstood your words? This confusion and distortion is a hallmark of the Leviathan spirit at work. Leviathan can twist a simple comment into something hurtful or offensive. In churches, it can cause disagreements and misunderstandings between members, leading to division and strife. By distorting communication, Leviathan breaks down trust and unity.

Leviathan thrives in division. This spirit seeks to bring division wherever there is unity, love, and cooperation. Leviathan causes tension and arguments in families, separating parents and children, as well as husbands and wives. In churches, it leads to splits and arguments among members, breaking the bond of fellowship. Division weakens people's ability to stand together, making them more vulnerable to other spiritual attacks. Leviathan does not want peace. Instead, it stirs up conflict, makes minor problems seem huge, and encourages people to focus on their differences rather than what unites them. It can even create bitterness and unforgiveness, which further deepens division. The Leviathan spirit is often hidden and subtle. It doesn't always show up in obvious ways, like a dramatic conflict. Instead, it slowly works behind the scenes, feeding on pride and misunderstandings, causing damage over time. You may not even realize it's at work until you start seeing the adverse effects in your relationships or community. Because it works subtly, Leviathan can be challenging to recognize. People might not think they are being influenced by pride or that their words are being twisted. This spirit operates quietly, waiting for the right moment to cause disruption, making it necessary for us to stay alert and spiritually aware. Although Leviathan was described as a sea creature in the Bible, its spiritual influence is real today. It affects individuals, families, churches, and even larger communities. We give Leviathan more power when we allow pride to take root in our hearts or let confusion and division go unchecked.

Characteristics and Manifestations

Pride and Arrogance: One of the most prominent characteristics of the Leviathan spirit is pride. Pride is the root of its power. This spirit often influences people to think too highly of themselves, to the point where they become arrogant and self-centered. A person under Leviathan's influence may refuse to admit they are wrong or fail to see their shortcomings. They may believe they are better than others and look down on those around them. Pride makes it difficult for people to humble themselves before God or seek help from others. This can lead to stubbornness, making them unwilling to listen to advice, correction, or wisdom from others. Proverbs 16:18 warns, "Pride goes before destruction and a haughty spirit before a fall." When pride takes hold, it sets a person up for failure, isolating them from God and those who can offer support.

Twisting of Words and Truth: Another manifestation of the Leviathan spirit is the twisting of words and truth. Just as Leviathan is described as a twisting serpent, this spirit takes words and turns them into something they were never meant to be. It distorts communication, making people misunderstand each other. A simple comment can be turned into a hurtful or offensive statement, leading to arguments and conflicts that should not have occurred. Leviathan confuses the truth, causing people to misinterpret intentions and escalate minor issues into major disputes. This twisting can cause bitterness and division in relationships because misunderstandings are never adequately addressed. It thrives in confusion and makes reconciliation more difficult, causing a deeper wedge between people.

Division and Strife: Leviathan works to divide and create strife wherever it goes. It can create tension between spouses, parents, and children in families. Minor disagreements can turn into major conflicts, with no one willing to compromise or see the other's perspective. In churches and communities, Leviathan causes division by pitting people against each other, often over minor issues that escalate due to pride and misunderstandings. Wherever unity and harmony are present, Leviathan seeks to break it. Division is a crucial goal for this spirit because it knows that when people are divided, they are weaker and less effective. A house divided against itself cannot stand (Mark 3:25), and Leviathan exploits this truth by driving wedges between people.

Unforgiveness and Bitterness: Leviathan loves to nurture unforgiveness and bitterness. When it causes misunderstandings and division, it works hard to ensure these conflicts remain unresolved. Unforgiveness keeps people trapped in anger and resentment, preventing them from healing or moving forward. Over time, this can turn into deep bitterness, poisoning the heart and destroying relationships. When people hold onto grudges and refuse to forgive, they allow Leviathan to maintain its influence. Forgiveness is essential to breaking free from Leviathan's grip because it removes the power of bitterness and strife. Ephesians 4:31-32 urges, "Let all bitterness and wrath and anger and clamor and slander be put away from you, along with all malice. Be kind to one another, tenderhearted, forgiving one another, as God in Christ forgave you."

Obstruction of Spiritual Growth: The Leviathan spirit also blocks spiritual growth. It often makes people feel stuck in their walk with God by keeping them focused on their pride or unresolved conflicts. When Leviathan influences a person, they may find it hard to pray, read the Bible, or grow spiritually. They may even experience spiritual stagnation, where they feel distant from God and unable to progress in their faith. This obstruction happens because Leviathan creates a wall of pride, preventing people from fully surrendering to God. It also keeps them from acknowledging their need for repentance or change, making spiritual growth impossible. Leviathan thrives when people are spiritually dry, feeding off their lack of connection with God.

Hardening of the Heart: Another manifestation is the hardening of the heart. When people are under Leviathan's influence, their hearts become rigid, making them unresponsive to God's voice and others. This hardening is often a result of pride, unforgiveness, or unresolved conflicts. A hardened heart makes it difficult for a person to feel compassion or humility, leading them further away from God and healthy relationships. A hardened heart also resists change, correction, and growth. It leads to a stubborn refusal to admit wrongs or to seek reconciliation. Over time, this hardening can lead to spiritual blindness, where a person no longer sees the truth about their situation or how they have been affected by Leviathan.

Disruptions in Relationships and Communities: Leviathan's influence is seen in the disruption of relationships. Whether in families, friendships, or churches, Leviathan works to tear apart the fabric of unity. It may start with minor issues that get blown out of proportion, leading to broken relationships that are difficult to repair. As long as pride, misunderstandings, and unforgiveness remain, Leviathan's influence will wreak havoc. In churches, this spirit can cause divisions between leadership and members, sow discord in small groups, and create an atmosphere of distrust. Its goal is to prevent the body of Christ from functioning in unity and love, weakening the church's witness and effectiveness.

Biblical References and Context

The Power and Majesty of Leviathan: One of the most detailed descriptions of Leviathan is found in the Book of Job. In this passage, God speaks to Job and describes Leviathan as a fearsome creature, impossible to tame or defeat by human strength. God uses Leviathan to symbolize His power and the limitations of man's abilities. The entire chapter highlights the immense strength, ferocity, and indomitable nature of Leviathan. Job 41:1-2 "Can you pull in Leviathan with a fishhook or tie down its tongue with a rope? Can you put a cord through its nose or pierce its jaw with a hook?" Job 41:10-11"No one is fierce enough to rouse it. Who then can stand against me? Who has a claim against me that I must pay? Everything under heaven belongs to me." Here, the Leviathan represents something beyond human control —whether a physical creature or symbolic of chaos and evil. It shows that only God can deal with such a force, emphasizing God's sovereignty and greatness.

Leviathan as a Symbol of Evil and Chaos: In Isaiah, Leviathan represents chaos and evil, which God will ultimately defeat. Isaiah

27:1: "In that day, the Lord will punish with his sword—his fierce, great and powerful sword—Leviathan the gliding serpent, Leviathan the coiling serpent; he will slay the monster of the sea." Here, Leviathan symbolizes the enemies of God, including nations and spiritual forces that stand in opposition to God's will. The coiling and gliding nature of Leviathan can be understood as symbolic of deceit, chaos, and destruction, much like how the Leviathan spirit operates in the spiritual realm, causing division, confusion, and rebellion.

Leviathan as a Defeated Enemy: In Psalm 74, Leviathan is referenced as God's past victories over chaotic forces. This psalm celebrates God's power in delivering His people from their enemies and highlights Leviathan as one of the defeated forces. Psalm 74:14: "It was you who crushed the heads of Leviathan and gave it as food to the creatures of the desert." God can defeat even the most fearsome of enemies, including Leviathan, which is seen as a symbol of chaos and destruction. God's authority over Leviathan reflects His ability to bring order and peace, even in uncontrollable or overwhelming situations.

Leviathan as Part of God's Creation: While Leviathan is often seen as a symbol of chaos or evil, Psalm 104 describes it as one of God's creations, playing a role in the natural world. This passage does not depict Leviathan as inherently evil but instead as part of the vastness and diversity of God's creation. Psalm 104:25-26 "There is the sea, vast and spacious, teeming with creatures beyond number—living things both large and small. There the ships go to and fro, and Leviathan, which you formed to frolic there." Leviathan represents the uncontrollable and mysterious aspects of God's creation. This passage reminds us that everything known and unknown is under God's control. While the Leviathan spirit may symbolize chaos, this psalm points to God's ultimate authority over all creation, including untamable forces.

Pharaoh and the Serpent: Though not explicitly called Leviathan, Pharaoh is compared to a great serpent in Ezekiel 29:3."Speak to him and say: 'This is what the Sovereign Lord says: I am against you, Pharaoh king of Egypt, you great monster lying among your streams. You say, 'The Nile belongs to me; I made it myself." Pharaoh's self-exaltation and pride mirror the arrogance that Leviathan embodies. God's judgment on Pharaoh reflects how He deals with prideful rulers and chaotic forces that oppose His will. This is an essential reference because it shows how Leviathan's characteristics can manifest in human leaders or systems that elevate themselves against God.

The Dragon and Satan: Though Leviathan is not directly mentioned in the Book of Revelation, the imagery of the dragon in Revelation 12:9 bears a striking resemblance to Leviathan. The dragon is described as Satan, the enemy of God, who seeks to deceive and destroy. Revelation 12:9: "The great dragon was hurled down—that ancient serpent called the devil, or Satan, who leads the whole world astray. He was hurled to the earth, and his angels with him." The dragon's role as a deceiver and agent of chaos aligns with how the Leviathan spirit operates. Like Leviathan, the dragon embodies pride, rebellion, and the twisting of truth, critical traits of the Leviathan spirit in spiritual warfare.

CHAPTER 2

SYMPTOMS
OF LEVIATHAN
INFLUENCE

Communication Breakdown: When communication breaks down, people often misunderstand each other's words, intentions, or feelings. This can happen when someone says something, but the other person interprets it entirely differently, leading to confusion. Misunderstandings can cause conflict, frustration, and hurt feelings, making it difficult for people to get along. If someone gives feedback, it might be seen as criticism. Instead of having a calm conversation, the person receiving the feedback might feel attacked and shut down emotionally. This makes it harder to resolve problems and build healthy relationships. Communication breakdowns can create a cycle where people stop listening to each other, making the situation worse.

Emotional Turmoil: When people go through emotional turmoil, they often feel overwhelmed by negative emotions like anger or frustration. These feelings can be directed at others or themselves, making life stressful and difficult. If someone holds onto bitterness from past hurts, it can affect their current relationships. They might find it hard to trust others or open up emotionally. This unresolved anger can create distance in relationships, leading to misunderstandings and heartache. Emotional turmoil can keep people stuck in unhealthy patterns, making it harder to heal and move forward.

Isolation and Withdrawal: Isolation happens when someone feels emotionally disconnected from others. They may withdraw from social interactions or relationships because they fear getting hurt or dealing with conflict. This can lead to feelings of loneliness and despair. When people isolate themselves, they miss relationships' support, love, and connection. Sometimes, they withdraw because they feel vulnerable or don't want to show their weaknesses. Over time, this isolation can make them feel even more disconnected, deepening their loneliness and making it harder to reach out for help.

Resistance to Change: Resistance to change is when someone refuses to be open or vulnerable with others, which blocks emotional intimacy and growth. Many people fear that they will seem weak if they let others in or admit they need help. This can lead to an unwillingness to share emotions or seek advice from others, keeping them stuck in the same unhealthy patterns. Sometimes, this resistance comes from pride—a belief that they can solve all their problems alone. However, this mindset can prevent people from getting the support they need to grow and heal. In relationships, resistance to change can create walls between people, making building trust and emotional connection difficult.

Critical Spirit: A critical spirit is when someone constantly finds fault with others, focusing more on their flaws than their strengths. Instead of offering encouragement, they highlight what's wrong or lacking, creating a hostile atmosphere in relationships and communities. If someone regularly criticizes others, they might push people away, causing tension and division. This attitude can make it hard to appreciate the good in others or life's circumstances, fostering a sense of dissatisfaction.

A critical spirit can harm relationships by making people feel judged and unappreciated rather than supported and valued.

Lack of Accountability: When people avoid taking responsibility for their actions, it shows a lack of accountability. This can be damaging, as it prevents personal growth and healing. People may refuse to admit their mistakes, instead blaming others for their problems. If someone shifts the blame onto others, they miss the opportunity to learn from their mistakes and grow stronger. This behavior can also harm relationships because it creates a sense of unfairness. If someone always avoids accountability, it can lead to unresolved issues and further conflict, making it hard to build trust and mutual respect.

How it Affects Families and Communities

The Leviathan spirit causes people to misinterpret each other's words and intentions. This leads to frequent misunderstandings, arguments, and conflicts that can tear families apart. Instead of discussing issues, individuals may withdraw, creating silence and emotional isolation within families and communities. The spirit can create an atmosphere of suspicion, where family members doubt each other's motives. This lack of trust can prevent open and honest communication. In larger communities, the Leviathan spirit can foster an environment where people distrust each other, leading to divisions and rivalries rather than unity and cooperation. Families may experience ongoing conflict as the Leviathan spirit stirs up anger and resentment. Minor issues can escalate into significant disagreements. When the Leviathan spirit is present, individuals may struggle to forgive past hurts. This can lead to long-standing grudges and emotional pain. Families and communities influenced by this spirit may develop a critical mindset, leading to constant criticism of one another. This fosters an unhealthy environment where people feel belittled and unappreciated. A culture of complaining and negativity can permeate families and communities, making it difficult for individuals to focus on positive aspects of life and relationships.

The Leviathan spirit can cause individuals to seek control over family dynamics, manipulating others to maintain power. This leads to unhealthy hierarchies and feelings of oppression. Family members may experience gaslighting, where their perceptions are questioned, making them doubt their feelings and experiences. This erodes their confidence and emotional well-being. The atmosphere created by the Leviathan spirit can lead to loneliness and disconnection among family members. Individuals may feel they cannot express themselves without fear of judgment or retaliation. In communities, individuals affected by the Leviathan spirit may withdraw from social activities, feeling disconnected from others and missing opportunities for connection and support. The Leviathan spirit can create a fear of vulnerability, preventing individuals from sharing their struggles or seeking help. This hinders personal growth and emotional healing. Families may become stuck in unhealthy patterns of behavior, unable to break free from cycles of conflict and dysfunction due to the influence of the Leviathan spirit. The effects of the Leviathan spirit can be passed down through generations. Children who grow up in an environment filled with conflict and distrust may replicate these behaviors in their relationships. In communities, the spirit can contribute to cultural norms prioritizing division and conflict, making it challenging for future generations to foster unity and cooperation.

Identifying Patterns of Behavior
Individuals influenced by the Leviathan spirit often respond defensively to even minor criticism. They may react with anger or denial instead of considering the feedback. A strong sense of pride can lead to difficulty acknowledging one's faults. People may refuse to apologize or take responsibility for their actions, creating relationship tension. Individuals may distort what others say, making it difficult to have clear conversations. This manipulation can lead to misunderstandings and confusion. The Leviathan spirit often uses guilt as a weapon. People may

manipulate others' feelings, making them feel responsible for problems or conflicts that are not theirs to bear. The Leviathan spirit fosters an environment where individuals see themselves in opposition to others. This division can occur within families or communities, leading to rivalries and conflict. Individuals may engage in gossip, spreading negative information about others. This behavior undermines trust and creates a toxic atmosphere.

The spirit can cause individuals to try to control situations and people around them, often out of fear of losing power or being vulnerable. People may struggle to express their true feelings or needs, fearing that doing so will expose them to rejection or manipulation. This leads to emotional distance and isolation. Those affected by the Leviathan spirit may avoid addressing conflicts directly, leading to unresolved issues and mounting resentment. Instead of addressing problems openly, individuals may express their frustrations indirectly, leading to confusion and ongoing tension. The Leviathan spirit can lead individuals to doubt themselves and their worth, causing them to seek validation from others in unhealthy ways. Some individuals may adopt a victim mentality, feeling powerless and blaming others for their problems. This can create a cycle of dependency and resentment. People influenced by the Leviathan spirit may withdraw from social interactions, feeling misunderstood or judged by others. Individuals may emotionally distance themselves from family and friends to protect themselves from potential hurt, leading to feelings of loneliness. The Leviathan spirit can lead to an environment of competition rather than collaboration, where individuals see others as threats rather than partners. People may constantly compare themselves to others, leading to feelings of envy and dissatisfaction. This can erode relationships and foster a toxic environment.

CHAPTER 3

FOUNDATIONS
FOR DEFEATING
LEVIATHAN

Psalm 74:14: "You crushed the heads of Leviathan; you gave him as food to the creatures of the wilderness." Recognizing God's power assures us that He can defeat any challenge we face, including the strongholds of the Leviathan spirit. As followers of Christ, we have been granted authority over spiritual forces. This verse encourages us to take a stand against the Leviathan spirit, knowing that God protects and empowers us. Paul urges believers to equip themselves with God's armor to withstand spiritual attacks. This preparation is vital for combating the Leviathan spirit and any other adversaries. Jesus emphasizes the necessity of prayer and fasting to overcome certain strongholds. Engaging in these spiritual disciplines strengthens our faith and allows us to seek God's guidance in defeating the Leviathan spirit. Prayer is a powerful tool for believers. It connects us with God and will enable us to intercede for ourselves and others, breaking the hold of the Leviathan spirit. Coming together in prayer and purpose strengthens our resolve against the Leviathan spirit. Supporting one another in the fight against spiritual adversaries is essential. We can encourage each other and stand firm against the Leviathan spirit.

God's Word guides us in our spiritual journey, providing wisdom and clarity as we navigate challenges posed by the Leviathan spirit. Submission to God and active resistance against the enemy is essential for overcoming the Leviathan spirit. This requires humility, repentance, and a commitment to living according to God's will. We are called to remain vigilant and steadfast in our faith, standing firm against the attacks of the Leviathan spirit.

The Authority of Scripture

2 Timothy 3:16-17: "All Scripture is breathed out by God and profitable for teaching, for reproof, for correction, and for training in righteousness, that the man of God may be complete, equipped for every good work." It is God's breath, meaning that it carries His authority. As a result, it is helpful in teaching and guiding us in our lives, helping us grow in our faith and understand His will. "Knowing this, first of all, that no prophecy of Scripture comes from someone's interpretation. For no prophecy was ever produced by the will of man, but men spoke from God as the Holy Spirit carried them along." This divine origin underlines the authority of Scripture in our lives. Psalm 119:160: "The sum of your word is truth, and every one of your righteous rules endures forever." The idea of infallibility means that Scripture is reliable and trustworthy. It does not lead us astray but guides us in the right direction. Inerrancy refers to the belief that the Bible, in its original manuscripts, is without error in all that it affirms, whether in matters of faith, morality, or history. Jesus emphasizes the enduring nature of God's Word. It stands firm against the changing tides of culture and human understanding. This assurance reinforces our confidence in Scripture as an unwavering guide. Psalm 119:105: "Your word is a lamp to my feet and a light to my path." Scripture illuminates our paths, providing clarity and direction in times of uncertainty. When facing spiritual challenges, such as resisting the Leviathan spirit, the Word of God helps us discern truth from deception. Acknowledging God's Word in our decision-making leads to

wisdom and understanding. By relying on Scripture, we align our lives with God's purposes, enabling us to navigate challenges effectively.

Ephesians 6:17: "And take the helmet of salvation, and the sword of the Spirit, which is the word of God." Paul describes the Word of God as the sword of the Spirit, highlighting its offensive and defensive role in spiritual warfare. It is our weapon against the lies and schemes of the enemy, including the Leviathan spirit. Each time Satan tries to deceive Him, Jesus responds with the truth of God's Word. This model demonstrates the authority of Scripture in overcoming spiritual attacks and resisting temptation. Romans 12:2: "Do not be conformed to this world, but be transformed by the renewal of your mind, that by testing you may discern what is the will of God, what is good and acceptable and perfect." Engaging with Scripture leads to transformation. As we read and meditate on God's Word, our minds are renewed, helping us to discern His will and resist influences that may lead us away from Him. The Word of God actively works in our lives, exposing our true thoughts and motives. This helps us align our hearts with God's desires and empowers us to live by His truth. Colossians 3:16: "Let the word of Christ dwell in you richly, teaching and admonishing one another in all wisdom, singing psalms and hymns and spiritual songs, with thankfulness in your hearts to God." Scripture fosters community and unity among believers. As we study and share God's Word, we grow in faith and encourage one another in our spiritual journeys. The early church centered their lives around the apostles' teachings, emphasizing the importance of Scripture in building strong, supportive communities of faith.

Prayer and Fasting as Weapons

Prayer is our direct line of communication with God. It allows us to express our thoughts, feelings and needs while listening for His guidance. In Philippians 4:6-7, Paul encourages us not to be anxious but to present our requests to God in prayer. Laying our concerns before Him not only brings peace but also opens the door for divine intervention in our lives. Through prayer, we exercise our authority as believers. Jesus teaches in Matthew 18:18, "Truly, I say to you, whatever you bind on earth shall be bound in heaven, and whatever you loose on earth shall be loosed in heaven." This authority empowers us to stand against spiritual forces and declare God's will over our lives and situations. Prayer also involves interceding for others. In James 5:16, "The prayer of a righteous person is powerful and effective." When we pray for others, we invite God's intervention into their lives, which can lead to healing, restoration, and freedom from oppressive spirits, including Leviathan.

Fasting is a spiritual discipline that involves abstaining from food or other comforts to focus on seeking God. It is often accompanied by prayer and serves as a way to demonstrate our dependence on Him. In Matthew 6:16-18, Jesus instructs His followers on how to fast, emphasizing that it should be done with humility and sincerity. Fasting helps us to refocus our minds and hearts on God. In Isaiah 58:6-9, God speaks through the prophet Isaiah about the true purpose of fasting. He desires a fast that releases the oppressed, shares food with the hungry and brings justice. This type of fasting draws us closer to God and aligns our hearts with His purposes. Fasting is a powerful tool for breaking spiritual strongholds. In Mark 9:29, Jesus explains that some demons can only be driven out through prayer and fasting.

When we combine prayer and fasting, we enter a deeper level of spiritual warfare. In Joel 2:12-13, God calls His people to return to Him with all their hearts, fasting, weeping, and mourning. This combined approach fosters a sincere and humble heart, enabling us to seek God's will more effectively. Engaging in prayer and fasting provides clarity and direction in decision-making. In Acts 13:2-3, the early church fasted and prayed before sending out Paul and Barnabas on their mission. This practice helped them discern God's calling and direction, ensuring their efforts aligned with His purposes. Both prayer and fasting contribute to spiritual renewal. In Matthew 4, we see Jesus fasting for forty days before beginning His ministry. During this time of preparation, they strengthened Him for the challenges ahead. Similarly, prayer and fasting prepare us for spiritual battles, renewing our strength and commitment to God.

Practical Steps for Prayer and Fasting

Setting Intentions: Setting clear intentions before beginning any fast is essential. Fasting is a spiritual discipline, not just a physical one, requiring you to consider your purpose. Take time to pray and seek God's guidance on what you should focus on during this period. Are you seeking freedom from the influence of the Leviathan spirit, clarity in a difficult situation, or a deeper relationship with God? By defining your goals before you start, you align your heart with God's purposes. During this time of reflection, ask God to reveal areas of your life that need healing or breakthrough. This could include struggles in relationships, overcoming pride, or breaking free from spiritual strongholds. By clearly identifying what you hope to achieve through the fast, you allow God to work more directly in those areas. Remember that fasting is not about making demands of God but about humbling yourself and being open to His will. Setting intentions helps you stay focused and motivated throughout the fast.

Choose the Type of Fast: Once you've set your intentions, the next step is to decide which fast is best for you. Different kinds of fasts exist, and what works for one person might not be suitable for another. A complete fast involves abstaining from all food, which is not always necessary or possible for everyone. A partial fast, where you give up certain foods or meals, can be just as powerful, especially if done with a sincere heart. You can also consider fasting from activities that consume your time and attention, like social media, television, or other distractions. The key is to choose something that will draw you closer to God. Whatever you decide to fast from, it should be something meaningful to you that challenges your flesh and shifts your focus from worldly distractions to spiritual growth. The goal is to create space for God in your life and allow Him to speak more clearly to you. It's essential to approach fasting with wisdom. Consider your physical and emotional health when deciding on the type of fast. If you have medical conditions, consult with a doctor before doing any drastic fasts. The most important thing is the heart behind the fast, not your chosen method.

Establish a Prayer Plan: Fasting without prayer is just skipping meals. Prayer is the fuel that powers your fast and connects you to God during this time of spiritual seeking. Before you begin, create a prayer plan to keep you focused and consistent. Set aside dedicated times daily to pray, meditate on Scripture, and listen for God's voice. Your prayer time should include worship, thanksgiving, intercession for others, and seeking God's guidance on the specific areas you've set intentions for. This time is meant to deepen your relationship with God, so prioritize it. You may want to start with a morning prayer, reflecting on what God is showing you, and end the day with another time of prayer and thanksgiving. Studying Scripture during your fast is essential as it helps you understand God's promises and truths. You may want to focus on Bible passages that address the areas you're fasting about, such as deliverance, humility, and the power of faith. As you fast, you'll find that your spiritual senses become sharper, and your prayer life becomes more focused and impactful. This is when you'll often hear God's voice more clearly and deeply feel His presence.

Seek Accountability: Fasting can be a physically and spiritually challenging experience. Having someone to support you can make a significant difference. Consider fasting with a friend, family member, or a small group. Sharing your journey with others provides encouragement and accountability, especially during challenging moments when you might be tempted to give up. When you fast with others, you can pray together, share insights, and lift each other. Fasting in the community helps you stay committed to your spiritual goals. Accountability partners can remind you of your intentions, offer encouragement when you feel weak, and celebrate victories with you. Even if you're fasting alone, it's a good idea to share your plans with a trusted friend or spiritual leader. They can pray for you, check in on you, and provide support during your fast. Knowing that others are standing with you in prayer and encouragement strengthens your resolve and helps you stay focused.

End with Gratitude: At the end of your fast, it's essential to reflect on the journey. Fasting is a time of spiritual growth, often bringing breakthroughs, clarity, and transformation. As you conclude your fast, pause to thank God for His presence, guidance, and lessons learned during this time. Take time to journal or reflect on how you've grown spiritually, what insights God has given you, and any prayers that have been answered. Consider how the experience has deepened your faith and how you can carry the lessons learned into your everyday life. Fasting should not be a one-time event but rather part of a continuous journey of spiritual growth. Ending with gratitude keeps your heart focused on God and His goodness. Reflect on how you can continue to pursue the goals set during the fast. Perhaps you've gained clarity about a specific area or experienced relationship healing. Whatever the outcome, commit to integrating the insights you've gained into your daily life, whether through regular prayer, studying the Word, or being more intentional in your relationships. Let the fast be a launching point for ongoing spiritual growth and a deeper connection with God.

Using God's Promises Against Leviathan

When facing the challenges and oppressive forces the Leviathan spirit represents, we must anchor ourselves in God's promises. The Scriptures provide powerful truths that remind us of His plans, protection, and presence. "For I know the plans I have for you," declares the Lord, "plans to prosper you and not to harm you, plans to give you hope and a future." (Jeremiah 29:11). In times of struggle, especially when facing manipulation, pride, and division —traits associated with the Leviathan spirit—we must remember that God has a plan for our lives that includes prosperity, hope, and a future. This assurance can help us resist feelings of despair and defeat that Leviathan seeks to instill. When we face opposition, we can remind ourselves that God's plans are protective. The Leviathan spirit may attempt to undermine our confidence or create chaos in our relationships. We can stand firm by trusting in God's promise, knowing He works for our good, even amidst adversity. The Leviathan spirit often brings discouragement and hopelessness. However, Jeremiah 29:11 assures us that our future is bright with hope. We can declare this promise over our lives and remind ourselves that God is orchestrating something good for us no matter how difficult our current circumstances may be. "God is our refuge and strength, an ever-present help in trouble." (Psalm 46:1). In times of spiritual attack, finding refuge in God is crucial. The Leviathan spirit can create turmoil and confusion, but Psalm 46:1 reminds us that God is a safe place where we can seek shelter. When we feel overwhelmed, we can retreat to Him through prayer and worship, allowing His peace to guard our hearts. The Leviathan spirit often thrives on our weaknesses and insecurities. Yet, this verse reassures us that God is our strength. When we feel powerless, we can lean into God's strength, knowing He empowers us to stand firm against any attack. This reliance on His strength enables us to resist the influence of Leviathan in our lives. Psalm 46:1 emphasizes God's constant presence. No matter where we are or what we face, God is there to help us. When the Leviathan spirit tries to isolate us or make us feel alone, we can take comfort in knowing that God is right there with us, ready to provide the help we need. When facing the Leviathan spirit, we can combat its influence by declaring and meditating on these promises. In moments of struggle, proclaim Speaking these truths out loud helps reinforce your faith and reminds you of God's plans and protection. Consider writing these verses on sticky notes and placing them in visible areas—on your mirror, fridge, or workspace. This constant reminder will help you focus on God's promises throughout your day. In your prayer time, take each promise back to God. Thank Him for His plans and express your trust in His protection. This dialogue deepens your relationship with Him and reinforces your faith. Share these promises with friends or family who may be struggling. Encouraging others with God's Word helps build a supportive community and reminds every one of His faithfulness.

CHAPTER 4

THE ROLE OF FAITH
IN COMBATTING
LEVIATHAN

F aith allows us to acknowledge that God has ultimate authority over all spiritual forces, including the Leviathan spirit. When we believe in God's power, we can confidently confront the lies and manipulations that Leviathan brings. Matthew 28:18, "All authority in heaven and on earth has been given to me," affirming that Jesus holds power over every spiritual entity. Our faith is strengthened when we trust in God's promises —knowing that God's plans for us are good and that He is our refuge and strength. This belief reassures us that God's power is far greater no matter how powerful Leviathan may seem. Faith draws us closer to God, allowing us to build a strong relationship. Regular prayer, worship, and studying Scripture foster this connection. The stronger our relationship with God, the more equipped we are to combat the Leviathan spirit, which often seeks to disrupt our intimacy with Him. When we face challenges, faith encourages us to seek God's guidance. In James 1:5, we are told, "If any of you lacks wisdom, you should ask God, who gives generously to all without finding fault."

Faith provides us with strength, especially when we feel weak or overwhelmed by the influences of Leviathan. 2 Corinthians 12:9, "My grace is sufficient for you, for my power is made perfect in weakness." Our faith in God can turn our vulnerabilities into opportunities for His strength to shine through; the Leviathan spirit often instills fear and doubt, attempting to paralyze us with insecurity. However, faith gives us the courage to confront these feelings. 2 Timothy 1:7, "God did not give us a spirit of fear but of power, love, and self-discipline." Faith thrives in the community. When we come together with fellow believers, we can encourage and strengthen one another in the fight against the Leviathan spirit. In Hebrews 10:24-25, we are called to "spur one another on toward love and good deeds, not giving up meeting together." This unity amplifies our faith and fortifies our resolve. Corporate prayer and worship are a powerful way to combat spiritual forces. When we gather together in faith, we create an atmosphere where God's presence can work mightily. In Matthew 18:20, Jesus assures us, "For where two or three gather in my name, there am I with them." This promise reinforces the power of united faith against the Leviathan spirit. Faith equips us to face challenges head-on. 1 John 5:4 reminds us that "everyone born of God overcomes the world." This victory extends to overcoming the negative influences of the Leviathan spirit. With faith, we can navigate complex situations and emerge victorious. Faith enables us to maintain hope, even in the face of adversity. The Leviathan spirit may attempt to sow despair, but our faith assures us that God is always at work. Romans 15:13, "May the God of hope fill you with all joy and peace as you trust in him." This joy and peace can guard our hearts and minds, keeping us steady against the chaos Leviathan seeks to create.

Building Unshakable Faith

Know God's Character: To build unshakable faith, we must first understand who God is. Psalm 100:5, "For the Lord is good, and his love endures forever," Knowing His character helps us trust Him more deeply. Reading and meditating on the Bible strengthens our understanding of God's character. Stories of His faithfulness, like those found in the lives of Abraham, Moses, and David, inspire us. When we see how God acted in their lives, we can be assured that He will act in ours, too.

Cultivate a Consistent Prayer Life: We can seek God's will for our lives through prayer. In Philippians 4:6-7, we are encouraged to present our requests to God, and His peace will guard our hearts. This peace is vital to unshakable faith, reassuring even in difficult times.

Engage in Worship and Praise: Worship shifts our focus from our problems to God's greatness. When we praise God, we declare His power and goodness. Psalm 34:1 says, "I will bless the Lord at all times; his praise shall continually be in my mouth." This continual praise strengthens our faith and reinforces our trust in God. Incorporating worship into our daily lives can help us build unshakable faith. This can include singing, listening to worship music, or even participating in church services. Surrounding ourselves with worship helps us remember God's faithfulness and presence.

Surround Yourself with Believers: Faith can grow more robust in the company of other believers. Hebrews 10:24-25 "Consider how we may spur one another on toward love and good deeds." By being part of a supportive community, we can encourage each other and share testimonies of God's goodness, which can strengthen our faith. Regular fellowship through small groups, Bible studies, or church activities allows us to share our struggles and victories. This interaction can provide accountability, support, and a sense of belonging, vital for maintaining unshakable faith.

Embrace Challenges as Opportunities: Challenges and trials are a part of life. Rather than viewing them solely as obstacles, we can see them as opportunities for growth. James 1:2-4 "Consider it pure joy... whenever you face trials of many kinds, because you know that the testing of your faith produces perseverance." This perspective helps us build resilience and strengthen our faith. When facing difficulties, we can rely on God's strength. Isaiah 40:31 states, "But those who hope in the Lord will renew their strength." We learn to lean on His promises and experience His faithfulness firsthand by trusting Him during tough times.

Practice Gratitude: Cultivating a heart of gratitude shifts our focus from what we lack to recognizing our blessings. 1 Thessalonians 5:18 encourages us to "give thanks in all circumstances." This practice helps us build unshakable faith by reminding us of God's goodness and faithfulness. Writing down things we are thankful for can help us remember God's past provisions and goodness. This simple act can serve as a reminder of His faithfulness, reinforcing our faith in times of doubt or struggle.

Stand Firm on God's Promises: Knowing and claiming God's promises is essential for building unshakable faith. Scriptures like Romans 8:28 remind us, "In all things, God works for the good of those who love him." We can maintain our faith by holding onto these truths, even when circumstances seem overwhelming. Creating personal affirmations based on scripture can help reinforce our faith. Regularly reciting these affirmations reminds us of God's promises, making standing firm in our beliefs easier.

Trusting God's Guidance
Trusting in God's guidance is a fundamental aspect of our faith journey. Knowing God is leading us can provide comfort and assurance in a world of choices, uncertainties, and challenges. Proverbs 16:3, "Commit to the Lord whatever you do, and he will establish your plans." The first part of this verse encourages us to commit our actions and decisions to God. This means bringing our plans, desires, and worries before Him. It involves surrendering our will to His and seeking His direction in everything we do. When we commit our plans to God, we acknowledge He knows what is best for us. The following promise

assures us that when we commit our ways to God, He will establish our plans. This means that God will guide and direct us, ensuring we are on the right path. It is a beautiful reminder that we are not alone in making decisions; God is actively involved in our lives.

Trusting God's guidance means recognizing that His wisdom far exceeds our own. While we may have our own ideas and plans, God sees the bigger picture and knows what is best for us. Life can be unpredictable, and sometimes we face decisions that seem overwhelming. When we trust in God's guidance, we can experience peace even in uncertainty. Philippians 4:6-7 encourages us not to be anxious but to present our requests to God. His peace will guard our hearts and minds. Regular prayer is essential for trusting God's guidance. We should pray over our decisions, asking for His wisdom and direction. James 1:5 reminds us that if we lack wisdom, we can ask God, who gives generously to all without finding fault. The Bible is full of knowledge and guidance for our lives. By studying Scripture, we can better understand God's character and His desires for us. When faced with decisions, we can look to God's Word for clarity and direction. Sometimes, seeking advice from trusted friends or mentors who share our faith can provide valuable insight. Proverbs 15:22, "Plans fail for lack of counsel, but with many advisers, they succeed." Discussing with others can help us gain perspective and discern God's guidance.

Trusting God's guidance requires action. Once we have sought His direction, we must be willing to obey what He reveals to us. This may involve stepping out of our comfort zone and trusting that God will lead us. God's guidance may lead us in unexpected directions. We must be open to His leading and willing to adjust our plans. Remembering that God's ways are higher than ours (Isaiah 55:8-9) can help us embrace change with faith. When we trust God's guidance, we can rest assured that He is in control. This assurance frees us from trying to figure everything out on our own. As we learn to trust God's guidance, our faith grows stronger. We begin to see His faithfulness in our lives, encouraging us to trust Him even more. Each step of obedience strengthens our relationship with Him.

Faith That Defies Logic

Faith involves a deep confidence in the things we hope for. This is not a vague wish but a firm assurance that what God has promised will pass. For instance, we may not see immediate results when we pray for healing, but our faith assures us that God hears our prayers and is at work. The second part of the verse emphasizes that faith also involves believing in things we cannot see. This can be challenging because we are often taught to rely on what we can see and understand. However, true faith goes beyond physical evidence. It recognizes that God operates in a realm that transcends our natural world. One of the most profound examples of faith that defies logic is the story of Abraham. God called Abraham to leave his homeland and go to a place he did not know (Genesis 12:1-3). This required immense faith, as Abraham had to trust God's promise without knowing where he was headed or how God would fulfill His promise of a great nation through him. Another powerful example is Moses leading the Israelites out of Egypt. When they reached the Red Sea, it seemed impossible to escape the pursuing Egyptians. Yet, Moses raised his staff, and God parted the waters (Exodus 14:21-22). This miraculous event demonstrates that faith often requires stepping into the unknown and trusting God to make a way, even when logic suggests otherwise. The story of Jericho's walls collapsing is another instance of faith that defies logic. God instructed the Israelites to march around the city for seven days, blowing trumpets and shouting. This strategy made little sense from a military perspective, yet their faith led to a miraculous victory (Joshua 6:1-20).

Isaiah 55:8-9 reminds us that God's thoughts and ways are higher than ours. What seems illogical to us may be part of God's perfect plan. Our understanding is limited, but God sees the entire picture and knows what is best for us. Faith that defies logic often serves to strengthen our relationship with God. When we trust Him in challenging situations, we experience His faithfulness, which deepens our reliance on Him. Each time we step out in faith, our trust strengthens, allowing us to face future challenges confidently. Regular prayer is essential for developing a solid faith. Prayer will enable us to communicate with God, express our hopes and fears, and seek His guidance. When we pray, we are reminded of God's promises and His ability to do the impossible. Studying the Bible reinforces our understanding of God's character and His promises. Stories of His faithfulness in Scripture inspire us to trust Him, even when things seem uncertain. Engaging with a community of believers can encourage us in our faith journey. Sharing testimonies of God's faithfulness and praying for one another helps to strengthen our resolve to trust in Him, even when logic suggests otherwise. When we step out in faith, we open ourselves to experiencing God's power in our lives. This can manifest in answered prayers, miraculous provisions, or unexpected blessings that affirm our faith. Faith that defies logic leads to a more profound relationship with God. As we trust Him with our uncertainties, we become more attuned to His voice and His leading in our lives. This intimacy enriches our spiritual walk and equips us to face challenges confidently.

CHAPTER 5

THE POWER OF
FORGIVENESS AND
RECONCILIATION

F orgiveness is the intentional decision to let go of feelings of resentment or vengeance toward someone who has wronged you. It does not mean that you condone the wrongdoing or that the relationship will immediately return to how it was before. Instead, grace releases you from the emotional burden of holding onto pain. The Bible teaches us about the importance of forgiveness in several passages. In Matthew 6:14-15, Jesus emphasizes that if we forgive others their trespasses, our Heavenly Father will also forgive us. This highlights the reciprocal nature of forgiveness—our willingness to forgive others opens the door for God's forgiveness. Reconciliation goes a step further than forgiveness. It involves restoring a broken relationship to a place of harmony and mutual understanding. Reconciliation requires both parties to work toward healing and rebuilding trust after a conflict or offense. The story of the Prodigal Son in Luke 15:11-32 illustrates the beauty of reconciliation. The father's willingness to forgive his wayward son and embrace him upon his return shows God's heart for us. Similarly, Joseph's reconciliation with his brothers after years of betrayal (Genesis 45) exemplifies the transformative power of forgiving and restoring relationships.

Forgiveness is a choice. It may not be easy, especially if the hurt runs deep, but consciously forgiving is a crucial step toward healing. This choice does not depend on the offender's apology or acknowledgment of wrongdoing. If appropriate, reaching out to the person who hurt you can be vital to the reconciliation process. Open and honest communication can help clear misunderstandings and rebuild trust. However, this step should be cautiously approached and only done when you feel ready. Reconciliation often requires time and effort to restore trust. This may involve establishing new boundaries and demonstrating through actions that the relationship can be safe and healthy again. It's essential to be patient, as rebuilding trust takes time and commitment from both parties. Forgiveness liberates us from the emotional burdens of anger and resentment. It allows us to move forward and find peace, improving mental health and emotional well-being. Reconciliation brings healing not just to individuals but also to families and communities. Restoring relationships can lead to a supportive environment where love and understanding thrive. When we practice forgiveness and reconciliation, we reflect God's grace. As we forgive others, we demonstrate the love and mercy that God has shown us, making us instruments of His peace in a broken world. Forgiving someone who has hurt you deeply can be one of the hardest things to do. It may take time, prayer, and support from others to navigate these feelings. It's important to be gentle with yourself during this process and to seek help if needed. Reconciliation often requires vulnerability. Opening yourself up to someone who has hurt you can be frightening, but it can also lead to deeper connections and healing. Trusting God to guide you in this process can provide the strength you need.

Breaking the Chains of Bitterness

Bitterness is a strong feeling of anger and resentment. It often arises when we feel wronged, betrayed, or mistreated. Instead of letting go of these feelings, we may cling to them, allowing them to grow and fester within us. The Bible warns us about the dangers of bitterness. Hebrews 12:15, "See to it that no one falls short of the grace of God and that no bitter root grows up to cause trouble and defile many." This verse reminds us that bitterness can spread and affect us and those around us. Bitterness is often rooted in unresolved emotional pain, and one of the most common ways it reveals itself is through constant feelings of anger, frustration, or sadness. When someone holds onto bitterness, they tend to focus on past hurts and wrongs, replaying these negative experiences in their minds over and over. This can make it difficult to move forward, as the emotional wounds feel fresh, even if the actual events happened long ago. You might feel a lingering sense of anger toward the person or situation that caused the hurt, but this emotion can also become generalized, spilling over into other areas of life. You may find yourself easily frustrated by things that wouldn't normally bother you, as the unresolved pain colors how you see the world. There may be moments of sadness, and feeling like you've been wronged or treated unfairly, leading to a victim mindset. This constant emotional turmoil can weigh heavily on your heart, making it hard to experience peace or joy.

Bitterness can also lead to an overwhelming sense of injustice, where you feel like life or others owe you something because of what you've been through. This feeling of unfairness can deepen the emotional wound, as you feel stuck in your pain, unable to let go of the past. The more you dwell on these feelings, the more they take root, making it harder to forgive or find healing. Often, these emotions can lead to a sense of isolation. You may feel like no one understands what you've gone through or how much you've been hurt. This can make it hard to connect with others emotionally, leaving you feeling alone, even when you're surrounded by people. The constant replaying of negative experiences can also prevent you from being fully present in your current relationships or enjoying new opportunities, as your mind is trapped in the past.

Bitterness doesn't just affect how you feel; it also impacts how you act toward others. One of the most common behavioral signs of bitterness is irritability. When someone is bitter, they tend to become easily annoyed or aggravated by others, even over minor things. You might snap at people more often or get upset more quickly than usual. This irritability can create tension in relationships, especially with those closest to you, like family members or friends. Withdrawing from relationships is another common behavioral sign. Bitterness can cause people to pull away from others, either because they don't want to risk getting hurt again or because they feel like others can't be trusted. You might start distancing yourself from people who care about you, avoiding social situations, or shutting down emotionally when others try to connect with you. Over time, this can lead to feelings of loneliness, as the walls you build to protect yourself from pain also keep love and support at a distance.

Bitterness can also make you more critical of others. You may focus on their flaws or mistakes rather than seeing their strengths or positive qualities. This critical attitude often stems from the hurt you're carrying, and it becomes a way to deflect your pain by pointing out the shortcomings of others. Unfortunately, this behavior can push people away and create a negative cycle of isolation and resentment. Bitterness can manifest in passive-aggressive behavior. Instead of addressing issues directly, you might express your frustrations through subtle jabs or indirect comments. This can further damage relationships, as it creates confusion and mistrust. The inability to communicate openly and honestly can cause misunderstandings, leaving others unsure of where they stand with you. Over time, bitterness can lead to a lack of empathy for others. When someone is consumed by their pain, it becomes harder to see or care about the needs and feelings of those around them. You might become more self-centered, focusing on your hurt rather than considering how your actions or words affect others. This emotional detachment can make it difficult to maintain healthy, meaningful relationships, as people begin to feel like you're no longer invested in their well-being.

The behavioral signs of bitterness create a vicious cycle. The more you withdraw or criticize others, the more isolated you become, which only deepens the feelings of anger, frustration, and sadness. The strain bitterness puts on relationships can also lead to more conflict, reinforcing the negative emotions you already feel. To break free from this cycle, it's important to recognize these behaviors and take steps toward healing and forgiveness. When emotional and behavioral signs of bitterness are left unchecked, they often feed off each other. Emotional turmoil like anger and sadness can lead to behaviors such as irritability, withdrawal, and criticism. In turn, these behaviors strain relationships and reinforce feelings of isolation and frustration, trapping you in a negative cycle. For example, dwelling on past hurts can make you feel more irritable and critical of others. As you criticize or distance yourself from loved ones, relationships become strained, leading to feelings of loneliness. This isolation then deepens the emotional pain, causing more bitterness to grow. It becomes harder to break free from the pattern because both your emotions and behaviors are working together to keep you stuck in a place of pain.

The Impact of Bitterness on Our Lives

Personal Well-Being: Bitterness, when left unchecked, can have serious effects on our mental and emotional health. Holding onto past hurts and refusing to let go of anger and resentment can cause constant stress and anxiety and even lead to depression. This happens because bitterness keeps us stuck in a negative emotional state. Whenever we think about the wrongs we've experienced, our bodies react with stress hormones, which can take a toll on our overall well-being. When we carry the burden of bitterness, it's like walking through life with a heavy weight. Feelings of resentment and anger often cloud the joy and peace God wants for us. Instead of experiencing the fullness of life, bitterness keeps us focused on the negative, robbing us of opportunities to enjoy the blessings around us. Unresolved emotions may overshadow simple moments that could bring happiness.

Over time, this constant emotional strain can make us feel drained, tired, and stuck in a cycle of negativity. Our minds become consumed with thoughts of how we've been wronged, and we replay past hurts in our heads, making it difficult to move forward. This emotional exhaustion can lead to feelings of hopelessness or depression because it becomes harder to see a way out of the pain. Bitterness also causes us to lose sight of the good in our lives, as it clouds our ability to focus on anything positive. Bitterness often affects how we think about ourselves. It can lead to feelings of self-pity or victimization, where we see ourselves as powerless or unfairly treated. This mindset can lead to low self-esteem and hinder personal growth because we become so focused on the wrongs we've experienced that we forget to look for ways to grow and heal. It is essential to release bitterness to protect our mental and emotional health. Letting go of past hurts doesn't mean that what happened is excused or forgotten, but it means freeing ourselves from the emotional burden that bitterness creates. When we forgive and move forward, we make room for joy, peace, and healing.

Relationships with Others: Bitterness doesn't just harm us personally; it also affects our relationships with others. When bitterness takes root in our hearts, it can poison our interactions with those around us. We may start to see people through the lens of past hurts, which can lead to misunderstandings, conflicts, and a lack of trust. One of the most damaging effects of bitterness is that it makes us more likely to misinterpret the words or actions of others. Because we still carry unresolved pain, we might read hostile intentions into situations where there are none. For example, someone may offer constructive criticism, but if we are bitter, we might see it as an attack or feel that they are out to hurt us. This defensiveness can lead to unnecessary conflicts and strain relationships.

Bitterness can also cause us to become overly critical of others. Instead of seeing the good in people, we tend to focus on their flaws, mistakes, or imperfections. This critical attitude can push others away, as they may feel judged or unappreciated. Over time, this can make it difficult to form deep, meaningful connections because trust and mutual respect are eroded by negativity. Another common effect of bitterness is withdrawal. When we feel hurt or resentful, we may distance ourselves from those around us to protect ourselves from further pain. This emotional withdrawal can cause loneliness, as the walls we build to keep others out also keep us from experiencing love, support, and connection. The more we isolate ourselves, the harder it becomes to rebuild relationships and find healing.

Bitterness also makes it challenging to communicate openly and honestly. When we are holding onto past hurts, we may avoid difficult conversations or refuse to express how we truly feel. This lack of communication can lead to further misunderstandings and deepen the divide between us and others. Bitterness can poison even the closest relationships, including those with family and friends. To nurture healthy and loving relationships, we must learn to let go of bitterness and practice forgiveness. By choosing to forgive, we create space for understanding, trust, and emotional intimacy to grow. This allows us to build stronger, healthier relationships based on love and mutual respect.

Spiritual Consequences: Bitterness not only affects our emotional well-being and relationships, but it also has spiritual severe consequences. In the Bible, we are called to forgive and let go of anger, as bitterness can create a barrier between us and God. Ephesians 4:31-32 says, "Get rid of all bitterness, rage, and anger," and instead encourages us to "be kind and compassionate to one another, forgiving each other, just as in Christ God forgave you." When we hold onto bitterness, we distance ourselves from

God's grace and love. This is because bitterness is rooted in unforgiveness, and God calls us to forgive as He has forgiven us. When we refuse to forgive, we allow anger and resentment to take hold of our hearts, blocking the flow of God's love and peace in our lives.

Bitterness can also hinder our spiritual growth. As we focus on the wrongs we've experienced, we become less focused on God and His will for our lives. Instead of trusting in God's ability to bring healing and justice, we may try to handle things independently, holding onto resentment rather than surrendering it to Him. This can prevent us from experiencing the fullness of God's peace and joy, as bitterness clouds our relationship with Him. Moreover, bitterness can cause us to become spiritually stagnant. We may find it difficult to pray, read the Bible, or seek God's presence when consumed by anger or hurt. This spiritual disconnect can make us feel distant from God, as our hearts become hardened by unforgiveness. The longer we hold onto bitterness, the more it grows, making it harder to experience God's grace and love.

To restore our relationship with God, it is essential to release bitterness through forgiveness. Forgiving others doesn't mean that what they did was right, but it means entrusting the situation to God and allowing Him to bring healing and justice in His time. When we forgive, we open our hearts to God's grace and allow His love to heal the wounds that bitterness has caused. Choosing to forgive and let go of anger is not always easy, but it is a crucial step in maintaining a healthy relationship with God. As we follow the example of Christ, who forgave us even when we didn't deserve it, we can experience the freedom and peace that comes from letting go of anger and resentment. Through forgiveness, we draw closer to God and open ourselves to His healing power, allowing His love to flow freely in our lives.

Breaking the Chains of Bitterness

Acknowledge the Hurt: The first step in breaking free from bitterness is to acknowledge the hurt. This means honestly facing the pain you feel instead of ignoring or suppressing it. Often, people hold onto bitterness because they haven't truly processed the hurt they've experienced. It's crucial to identify the source of the bitterness. Ask yourself, what caused this hurt? Who hurt me? How has this affected my emotions and behavior? This self-reflection can be difficult because it requires confronting painful memories or experiences. However, acknowledging the hurt is an important step toward healing. By doing this, you give yourself permission to feel and understand the depth of your emotions, which helps you begin the process of letting go. In some cases, it might be helpful to talk to someone you trust, like a friend or counselor. Sometimes, just verbalizing your pain helps bring clarity. Sharing your feelings with a trusted person can provide emotional support and allow you to see your situation from a fresh perspective. It may also offer guidance on handling the emotions you are processing.

Make the Choice to Forgive: Forgiveness is a powerful tool for breaking free from bitterness. It is not about excusing the wrong done to you or pretending it didn't hurt. Rather, forgiveness is a conscious decision to release bitterness's hold over your heart. When you choose to forgive, you let go of the anger and resentment that weigh you down. Forgiveness is more about your healing than the person who hurt you. By holding onto bitterness, you are allowing the actions of others to control your emotional state. But when you forgive, you regain that control and free yourself from the emotional burden. It's important to understand that forgiveness is not a one-time decision. It's a process that may need to be revisited multiple times, especially if the hurt runs deep. There might be moments when you feel the sting of bitterness again, but in those moments, remind yourself of your choice to forgive and continue moving forward in your healing.

Seek God's Help: Forgiveness and healing from bitterness can be difficult, but God offers us His strength when we feel weak. Turning to God in prayer is an essential part of the process. Ask God to give you the strength to forgive, to soften your heart, and to help you let go of bitterness. Psalm 34:18 says, "The Lord is close to the brokenhearted and saves those who are crushed in spirit." This verse reminds us that God is near when we are hurting. He understands our pain, and He is always willing to help us heal. When you feel overwhelmed by your emotions, remember that you don't have to face them alone. God is with you, ready to comfort and guide you. In your prayers, be honest with God about how you feel. If you're struggling to forgive, ask Him to help you in that process. As you surrender your pain to Him, trust that He is working in your heart to bring healing and peace.

Focus on Gratitude: Bitterness often thrives when we focus on the negative aspects of our lives or the wrongs that have been done to us. One way to counteract bitterness is by shifting your focus to gratitude. Practicing gratitude helps you see the good in your life, which can change your perspective and lessen feelings of bitterness. Make it a habit to write down things you are thankful for each day. Even small blessings like a beautiful sunset, a kind word from a friend, or good health are reasons to be grateful. This practice can help you develop a more positive mindset, which makes it harder for bitterness to take root in your heart. Gratitude also opens the door to healing because it shifts your focus away from the pain of the past and towards the blessings of the present. As you make gratitude a daily practice, you may find that your heart becomes lighter, and you experience more joy.

Surround Yourself with Positive Influences: The people you surround yourself with can have a significant impact on your emotional health. Engage with people who uplift and encourage you. Spending time with individuals who are constantly negative or critical can reinforce feelings of bitterness. But connecting with people who embody kindness, forgiveness, and positivity can inspire you to let go of anger and pursue emotional healing.

Seek out friends or family members who encourage you to be the best version of yourself—those who listen with compassion and offer support without judgment. Positive relationships can provide strength and encouragement, especially when struggling with bitterness or hurt. Sometimes, healing from bitterness may also mean setting boundaries with people who contribute to your negativity or may have been part of the hurt you've experienced. Protecting your emotional well-being is essential as you seek healing.

Embrace Healing: Healing from bitterness is not an overnight process; it is a journey that requires patience and grace. Being kind to yourself is important as you work through your emotions. Some days will be more complex than others, and that's okay. What matters is that you are making progress toward emotional freedom. During this journey, engage in activities that promote your emotional and spiritual well-being. Spend time in prayer, meditate on Scripture, or simply take time to reflect on nature. These activities can help you connect with God, find peace, and center your emotions. As you make progress, celebrate your growth. Every step you take towards letting go of bitterness is a victory. Acknowledge how far you've come and trust that God is guiding you through healing.

The Victory of Forgiveness

Healing Our Hearts: Holding onto grudges and resentment can be a heavy burden on both our emotional and spiritual well-being. Unforgiveness often leads to bitterness, anger, and emotional pain, creating turmoil in our lives. When we harbor negative feelings, we trap ourselves in a cycle of hurt, continuously revisiting the pain caused by past wrongs. This emotional baggage can lead to stress, anxiety, and even physical health issues, as the weight of unforgiveness affects every part of our being. However, when we choose to forgive, we take a significant step toward healing. Forgiveness is like unlocking a door that has kept us bound to our pain, allowing us to walk in freedom. By releasing grudges, we allow God to enter into those broken areas of our hearts and begin the healing process. In Psalm 147:3, "He heals the brokenhearted and binds up their wounds." This reminds us that God is the ultimate healer but needs us to open our hearts to His healing through forgiveness. Healing our hearts through forgiveness also allows us to experience the joy and peace God desires. Romans 15:13 says, "May the God of hope fill you with all joy and peace as you trust in him, so that you may overflow with hope by the power of the Holy Spirit." When we forgive, we free ourselves from the emotional bondage that hinders our ability to experience God's love and peace fully. The process of forgiveness helps us shed the bitterness that weighs us down, making room for joy and peace to take root in our hearts.

Restoring Relationships: Forgiveness is vital to repairing relationships damaged by hurt, betrayal, or misunderstanding. Holding onto unforgiveness often creates a barrier between us and those we care about. It prevents healing and reconciliation, causing relationships to become strained or even broken. By forgiving, we dismantle those barriers and create an opportunity for trust to be rebuilt. When we forgive someone wronged us, we open the door for reconciliation. This doesn't mean that the relationship will automatically return to what it was before, but it does create space for healing and a new beginning. Forgiveness allows for honest conversations, apologies, and understanding to take place. These moments of vulnerability can bring people closer, fostering stronger connections built on mutual respect and grace. It's important to remember that forgiveness is not a one-sided act. It's part of a process that involves both giving and receiving. Sometimes, in our relationships, we need to seek forgiveness from others for the harm we've caused, whether intentionally or unintentionally. This act of humility can repair relationships, as it demonstrates a desire to restore trust and heal wounds. The Bible encourages us to pursue reconciliation. In Matthew 5:23-24, "Therefore, if you are offering your gift at the altar and there remember that your brother or sister has something against you, leave your gift there in front of the altar. First, go and be reconciled to them; then come and offer your gift." This passage highlights the importance of restoring relationships and emphasizes that God values reconciliation.

Reflecting God's Love: Forgiveness is one of the most potent ways we reflect God's love to others. As followers of Christ, we are called to imitate His character, and one of the most defining aspects of God's nature is His abundant grace and mercy. When we forgive others, we are extending the same grace and love that God has freely given us. This act of grace is a tangible expression of God's love, and it reveals His heart to those around us. In Ephesians 4:32, "Be kind and compassionate to one another, forgiving each other, just as in Christ God forgave you." This verse underscores that our ability to forgive is directly tied to the forgiveness we have received from God. We forgive because we have been forgiven. God, in His infinite mercy, has forgiven us of our sins, no matter how great or small. As recipients of such overwhelming grace, we must pass it on to others. Forgiving others is a reflection of the Gospel itself. The very foundation of our faith is rooted in forgiveness—Jesus died on the cross to forgive our sins and reconcile us to God. When we forgive, we live out the message of the cross daily. It's a reminder to others that God's love is transformative and that He desires healing and reconciliation for all His children. Moreover, when we forgive, we show others that God's love transcends human flaws and failings. People are imperfect, and we all make mistakes that hurt others, but God's love remains constant. By extending forgiveness, we demonstrate that His love is more significant than any offense and that His mercy has the power to heal brokenness. Forgiveness is not always easy, but it is a testament to the depth of God's love working in us and through us.

The Healing Power of Forgiveness: Forgiveness brings spiritual healing as well. When we hold onto resentment, we create a barrier between ourselves and God. Unforgiveness can harden our hearts and make it difficult to experience the fullness of God's grace and love. It also disrupts our relationship with God, as harboring bitterness goes against His command to forgive. Jesus made it clear that forgiveness is essential for those who follow Him. In Matthew 6:14-15, "For if you forgive other people when they sin against you, your heavenly Father will also forgive you. But if you do not forgive others their sins, your Father will not forgive your sins." Forgiveness is not optional; it's a command that comes with both blessings and consequences. By choosing to forgive, we keep our hearts open to the forgiveness and grace that God extends to us. Forgiveness frees us from the bondage of bitterness and anger. These negative emotions can consume our thoughts and energy, robbing us of joy, peace, and spiritual growth. When we forgive, we release the emotional burden that bitterness brings and open ourselves to spiritual renewal. Our hearts become more attuned to God's will, and we can experience His presence more fully.

The Power of Hope

Hope in Difficult Times: Forgiveness brings hope, particularly when bitterness and resentment might seem to offer temporary comfort or a false sense of control. When we choose to forgive, we open the door to healing and restoration, making room for hope to flourish. In moments of pain, hurt, or betrayal, it's easy to become consumed by negative emotions, allowing bitterness to take root. But forgiveness is the pathway to freeing ourselves from these chains, allowing us to experience hope, joy, and peace, even amid hardship. Romans 15:13, "May the God of hope fill you with all joy and peace as you trust in him, so that you may overflow with hope by the power of the Holy Spirit." As we place our trust in Him and follow His guidance, He fills our hearts with the joy and peace that surpasses our circumstances. Even when life feels overwhelming, choosing to forgive those who have wronged us can bring renewed hope, knowing that God is at work within us to heal and restore. In difficult situations, unforgiveness can become a heavy burden. It weighs down our hearts, draining our energy and making it hard to see any way forward. However, when we let go of resentment, we release ourselves from this burden and open the way for hope to re-enter our lives. Forgiveness allows us to stop dwelling on the past and move forward with a sense of purpose and renewed optimism. Hope thrives in forgiveness because when we forgive, we trust in God's ability to make things right, even when we can't. Forgiveness doesn't mean forgetting or excusing the wrong done to us, but it means trusting that God will bring justice, healing, and reconciliation in His time. This trust in God's more excellent plan for our lives enables us to experience hope, even when the situation seems hopeless. By surrendering our pain and anger to Him, we allow God to work in ways we might not have imagined, bringing about transformation, healing, and renewed relationships.

The Role of the Holy Spirit: Forgiveness is not an easy process, and it often feels impossible to forgive those who have deeply hurt us. This is where the Holy Spirit's power becomes essential. In Romans 15:13, "overflow with hope by the power of the Holy Spirit." The ability to forgive does not come from our strength; the Holy Spirit gives us the courage, strength, and grace to let go of bitterness and embrace forgiveness. The Holy Spirit is our helper and guide in this process, reminding us of the love and grace we have received through Christ and empowering us to extend that same grace to others. In John 14:26, "But the Advocate, the Holy Spirit, whom the Father will send in my name, will teach you all things and remind you of everything I have said to you." The Holy Spirit works in us, teaching us the importance of forgiveness and reminding us of Christ's example. He helps us to release feelings of anger, resentment, and revenge, and instead, empowers us to choose love, compassion, and grace. Without the help of the Holy Spirit, forgiveness can feel impossible. Anger and bitterness can grip our hearts so tightly that it seems there is no way to break free. However, the Holy Spirit is our source of strength, enabling us to overcome these feelings. Galatians 5:22-23 tells us that the fruit of the Spirit includes love, peace, patience, kindness, goodness, faithfulness, gentleness, and self-control—all qualities we need to forgive others. As we lean into the Spirit, He produces these fruits, allowing us to forgive with genuine love and grace. The Holy Spirit empowers us to forgive and gives us wisdom and discernment. He helps us to navigate the complexities of relationships and offenses. Sometimes, forgiveness might require setting healthy boundaries, and the Holy Spirit guides us in making those decisions in love rather than anger. His presence in our lives ensures that forgiveness does not come at the cost of our well-being, but rather, in alignment with God's will for our healing and peace.

When we cannot forgive, the Holy Spirit intercedes on our behalf. Romans 8:26 says, "Similarly, the Spirit helps us in our weakness. We do not know what we ought to pray for, but the Spirit himself intercedes for us through wordless groans." When the weight of unforgiveness feels too heavy, the Holy Spirit comes alongside us, interceding with prayers for our healing and strength. He helps us pray even when we feel lost in our hurt and pain. Through the power of the Holy Spirit, we can let go of past hurts and embrace forgiveness. The Spirit not only equips us with the tools we need to forgive but also helps us understand the deep spiritual significance of forgiveness. Just as Christ forgave us through the power of the Spirit, we are called to forgive others through that same power. This brings us back to the heart of the Gospel: the forgiveness we receive through Jesus Christ is the foundation for our ability to forgive others.

Overflowing with Hope and Healing: When we walk in forgiveness, we overflow with hope because we align ourselves with God's will for our lives. We are no longer trapped in the cycle of bitterness and pain; instead, we experience freedom, peace, and joy. This hope comes not from our strength, but from the transforming work of the Holy Spirit within us. As we forgive, we reflect the heart of God and experience the fullness of life that

He has promised us. As we trust in God and rely on the power of the Holy Spirit, we can face even the most difficult circumstances with hope. Forgiveness frees us from the chains of resentment, and with that freedom comes the ability to experience the joy, peace, and healing that God has in store for us. We can rest in the assurance that God is working all things together for our good, and that He will bring about restoration and renewal in His perfect timing.

The Joy of Forgiveness

Forgiveness is one of the most liberating acts we can ever perform. When we choose to forgive, we experience a profound sense of freedom, where the heavy chains of bitterness, anger, and resentment disappear. Holding onto grudges can feel like carrying a constant weight on our hearts—one that burdens us emotionally, mentally, and spiritually. However, by extending forgiveness, we free ourselves from these chains and open our hearts to a life filled with joy, peace, and spiritual renewal. Bitterness and resentment not only hurt us internally, but they also cloud our ability to experience the fullness of life that God desires for us. They create walls that separate us from peace, making it difficult to enjoy the blessings that are right in front of us. When we forgive, those walls come down, allowing us to walk in a new sense of freedom. This freedom is not simply the absence of pain but the active presence of joy, hope, and emotional lightness. Romans 15:13 says, "May the God of hope fill you with all joy and peace as you trust in him, so that you may overflow with hope by the power of the Holy Spirit." This verse captures the essence of the freedom that comes from forgiveness. Trusting in God is key to the process of letting go of anger and releasing the hold of bitterness. When we choose to forgive, we place our trust in God's justice, mercy, and timing, believing that He will handle the wrongs that have been done to us. This act of trust allows us to experience the "joy and peace" that Romans speaks of—an inner calm that surpasses our circumstances and fills us with hope.

In addition to spiritual freedom, forgiveness brings emotional and mental freedom. The negative emotions that come with harboring bitterness can affect our mental health, leading to stress, anxiety, and even depression. When we forgive, we release these negative emotions, and in doing so, we create space for positivity to flow into our lives. By choosing to forgive, we no longer allow the past to define our present or control our future. We reclaim the ability to focus on the good things in life, embracing peace, joy, and contentment. Forgiveness also brings physical freedom. Numerous studies have shown that holding onto anger and bitterness can negatively affect our health, contributing to problems like high blood pressure, weakened immune systems, and chronic stress. When we forgive, we free our bodies from the toxic effects of long-term anger, allowing us to live healthier, more vibrant lives. The freedom that comes with forgiveness is not limited to a single moment. It is an ongoing process that brings lasting peace and joy. As we continue to forgive—whether forgiving someone once for a deep hurt or choosing daily to forgive the minor irritations that life brings— we experience a more profound sense of freedom with each step. Forgiveness becomes a way of life that leads us to walk in greater joy and emotional wholeness.

Forgiveness is not just a personal experience; it is a gift that can transform the lives of those around us. As we embrace forgiveness and experience its freedom, we naturally inspire others to follow suit. The power of forgiveness can create a ripple effect that touches our hearts and those in our families, communities, and beyond. When we choose to forgive, we break the cycle of bitterness. In many cases, resentment and anger are passed from one person to another—hurts are inflicted, and new hurts are created in response. This cycle can continue indefinitely, with pain growing and spreading like wildfire. However, forgiveness interrupts this cycle. By choosing to forgive, we stop the cycle of bitterness and replace it with love, understanding, and grace. This act of forgiveness can heal relationships that may have been fractured for years, bringing restoration and reconciliation where there was once only division. Forgiveness inspires forgiveness. When we forgive others, it sets an example that others can follow. People often hesitate to forgive because they fear it will make them appear weak or lose their sense of justice. However, when we model forgiveness, we show others it is an act of strength, courage, and faith. Our willingness to forgive encourages others to relinquish their grudges and take the same steps toward freedom. This ripple effect can spread throughout families, churches, workplaces, and communities, creating an atmosphere of healing and reconciliation. Matthew 18:21-22, "Lord, how many times shall I forgive my brother or sister who sins against me? Up to seven times?" Jesus answered, "I tell you, not seven times, but seventy-seven times." This teaching reminds us that forgiveness is not a one-time act but a continuous process of grace. As we continually forgive, we spread the message that forgiveness is a daily practice that has the power to transform relationships and communities. Just as Christ forgives us endlessly, we are called to forgive others, offering them the same grace and mercy we have received. One of the most profound ways forgiveness can transform a community is by restoring broken relationships. Whether it's a family feud, a long-standing disagreement between friends, or a conflict within a church, forgiveness has the power to bring healing and unity. When we forgive, we open the door for reconciliation, rebuilding trust, and strengthening bonds. In families, forgiveness can heal generational wounds, bringing renewed love and understanding between parents and children, siblings, or spouses. In churches, forgiveness can unite a divided congregation, allowing the body of Christ to function in harmony and love. Forgiveness can also be a witness to the world. In a culture that often promotes holding grudges and seeking revenge, the act of forgiving can stand out as a powerful testimony of God's love and grace. When we forgive, we demonstrate the character of Christ, showing others that forgiveness is not only possible but transformative. Our forgiveness can reflect the Gospel itself—the message that Christ forgave us, even while we were still sinners, and calls us to do the same for others.

The gift of forgiveness can potentially create a ripple effect that extends far beyond our immediate circumstances. As we forgive and encourage others to forgive, we contribute to healing the world around us. Every act of forgiveness is a step toward a more compassionate, loving, and understanding community. Whether within our families, neighborhoods, or workplaces, forgiveness builds bridges of reconciliation and peace. Forgiveness strengthens relationships. We create opportunities for deeper connections and stronger bonds when we forgive those who have hurt us. Forgiveness allows us to move past misunderstandings, arguments, and disappointments, opening the door for healing conversations and meaningful interactions. As relationships are restored, trust is rebuilt, and love can flourish again. By embracing forgiveness, we also set a powerful example for future generations. Children who grow up in environments where forgiveness is practiced learn the value of grace and compassion. They see firsthand forgiveness's impact on relationships and are more likely to carry those values into their own lives. In this way, the gift of forgiveness continues to bless and transform future generations, creating a legacy of love, peace, and reconciliation.

Healing Broken Relationships

Broken relationships can be one of life's most painful experiences. The emotional scars can run deep, whether it's a rift with a family member, a falling out with a friend, or struggles in a romantic partnership. However, the good news is that healing is possible through forgiveness, communication, and God's grace. This section explores how we can mend broken relationships and restore connections that once brought joy and love. One of the primary reasons relationships break down is miscommunication.

Words can be misunderstood, intentions can be misinterpreted, and assumptions can lead to conflict. When people do not express their feelings or thoughts openly, misunderstandings can fester and grow. Sometimes, one person may unintentionally hurt another's feelings. This can happen through careless words, actions, or decisions. If not addressed, these hurt feelings can create distance and resentment. Trust is a foundational element of any relationship. It can be challenging to rebuild when trust is broken—whether through betrayal, dishonesty, or unfaithfulness. Without trust, relationships often struggle to thrive. Life events such as job loss, illness, or financial troubles can strain relationships. Stress can cause individuals to react negatively, leading to conflict and misunderstandings.

The Importance of Healing

One of the most important aspects of healing is the restoration of peace. When relationships are damaged, the turmoil and unresolved conflict can lead to ongoing emotional and spiritual pain. Bitterness, anger, and resentment often settle into our hearts when conflicts are left unresolved. This can disrupt the relationship in question and our overall sense of well-being. When we actively seek healing in our relationships, we are choosing to restore peace in our lives. The Bible encourages us to be peacemakers, as stated in Matthew 5:9, "Blessed are the peacemakers, for they will be called children of God." Healing broken relationships allows us to create an environment where peace, love, and understanding thrive. Without peace, it becomes challenging to maintain a healthy emotional and spiritual balance, and we are left feeling burdened by the weight of unresolved conflict. Peace is the fruit of healing, bringing a sense of calmness and harmony to our hearts and minds. It allows us to experience joy and contentment without being haunted by past hurts. Healing broken relationships leads to the freedom to move forward, unshackled by emotional baggage. Restoring peace is foundational because it allows for clarity of mind, emotional freedom, and reconnection with those we love.

Healing is not just about mending relationships but also about fostering personal growth. When we face the brokenness of a relationship and take steps toward healing, we open ourselves to learning valuable lessons about communication, empathy, patience, and forgiveness. Each relationship brings unique challenges, and healing from those challenges helps us grow emotionally, mentally, and spiritually. Healing teaches us the power of communication. Many conflicts arise from misunderstandings, unmet expectations, or ineffective communication. In the healing process, we learn the importance of expressing our thoughts and feelings openly and honestly while listening to the other person. Healthy communication is at the heart of all relationships, and when we commit to healing, we commit to improving this vital skill. Empathy is another crucial lesson that comes from the healing process. When we seek to heal relationships, we are challenged to put ourselves in the other person's shoes. This requires us to step outside of our hurt and consider how others might feel. Empathy deepens our understanding of others and softens our hearts toward those who may have wronged us. It also allows us to approach conflicts with more compassion and humility, fostering an atmosphere where healing can occur. Forgiveness is perhaps the most difficult yet most rewarding aspect of healing. As we work toward healing broken relationships, we learn that forgiveness is not just about excusing someone's actions but about releasing the power that those actions have over us. Forgiveness helps us let go of bitterness, resentment, and anger. It allows us to move past the pain and choose love over vengeance. The ability to forgive is a powerful indicator of personal growth, as it shows that we are maturing emotionally and spiritually. The Bible encourages us to grow in our relationships and to strive for reconciliation. Colossians 3:13, "Bear with each other and forgive one another if any of you has a grievance against someone. Forgive as the Lord forgave you." This verse reminds us that healing, forgiveness, and reconciliation are essential to our spiritual growth. When we heal, we mature, becoming more Christlike in interacting with others.

As Christians, we are called to reflect God's love in every aspect of our lives, including our relationships. Healing broken relationships is a personal victory and a reflection of God's grace and mercy. How we approach healing and reconciliation speaks volumes about the love we have received from God and the transformative power of that love. God's love is vital. His love reaches into the broken parts of our lives and mends them with grace and compassion. As followers of Christ, we are called to extend that same grace to others, especially in times of conflict. Healing broken relationships is one of the most profound ways to demonstrate God's love to the world. It shows that we are willing to forgive as we have been forgiven and to love as we have been. John 13:34-35, "A new command I give you: Love one another. As I have loved you, so you must love one another. By this, everyone will know that you are my disciples if you love one another." Healing our relationships is an expression of this command. When we seek reconciliation, we show that our love is not conditional on perfection but is rooted in the grace that God has given us. It is a testimony to the transforming power of God's love. Moreover, healing broken relationships can be a powerful witness to others. In a world where division, grudges, and hostility are standard, choosing to heal and reconcile stands out as a radical act of love. When people see Christians actively working to heal their relationships, they witness the power of God at work. It demonstrates that the love of Christ is more potent than hurt, betrayal, or conflict. Healing becomes an opportunity to showcase the redemptive power of the Gospel in our lives. It's essential to recognize that healing is a journey, not a one-time event. The process of healing broken relationships takes time, effort, and patience. Some hurts may be deep and require ongoing work toward reconciliation. Other conflicts may be resolved more quickly, but commitment to maintaining healthy relationships is still required. No matter how long the process takes, the key is to keep moving forward, trusting that God is working in the situation to bring about restoration. Along this journey, we are not alone. God promises to be with us, guiding us through healing. He provides strength when the road is difficult and wisdom when we are unsure of the next steps. Philippians 4:7 reminds us that God's peace, which surpasses all understanding, will guard our hearts and minds as we seek healing and reconciliation.

Steps to Heal Broken Relationships

Acknowledge the Issue: The first and most crucial step in healing a broken relationship is acknowledging a problem. Ignoring the issue or pretending it doesn't exist will not lead to healing. Avoidance can create even more distance between individuals, leading to deeper emotional wounds. Denial keeps the problem festering under the surface, causing further damage over time. To start healing, you must be honest about the situation and the emotions involved. This requires introspection and a willingness to face uncomfortable truths. What caused the rift in the relationship? Was it a misunderstanding, unmet expectations, or hurtful actions? Acknowledging the root of the problem allows both parties to see what needs to be addressed. The Bible emphasizes the importance of dealing with issues rather than allowing them to simmer. Ephesians 4:26-27, "In your anger do not sin: Do not let the sun go down while you are still angry, and do not give the devil a foothold." This verse encourages us to promptly address conflicts without letting them linger.

Open Communication: Once the issue is acknowledged, the next step is to communicate openly and honestly. Communication is the cornerstone of any healthy relationship, and it also plays a vital role in healing. Approach the conversation with kindness, humility, and a genuine desire to understand the other person's perspective. During this conversation, it's essential to express your feelings without placing blame. One helpful technique is to use "I" statements, such as "I feel hurt when…" or "I felt misunderstood when…" This approach allows you to share your emotions without accusing the other person or making them feel defensive. For example, instead of saying, "You never listen to me," you could say, "I feel unheard when my thoughts are interrupted." In addition to expressing your feelings, be willing to listen to the other person actively. Listening without interrupting allows the other person to feel heard and valued. Active listening also helps clarify any misunderstandings that may have contributed to the conflict. Communication should be two-way, with both parties sharing openly and listening attentively. James 1:19 reminds us of the importance of communication, saying, "Everyone should be quick to listen, slow to speak, and slow to become angry." Open, compassionate communication sets the stage for healing and understanding.

Offer and Seek Forgiveness: Forgiveness is the key to unlocking the door to healing. Without forgiveness, it is impossible to mend a broken relationship fully. Both parties must be willing to offer forgiveness for any wrongs that have been done, as well as seek forgiveness for their own mistakes. Forgiveness is a conscious choice that allows us to release feelings of bitterness, resentment, and anger. It doesn't mean that the hurt never happened, but it does mean that we are choosing not to let the hurt define the relationship moving forward. Forgiving someone can be difficult, especially when the pain runs deep, but it is essential for healing. In addition to offering forgiveness, be open to seeking forgiveness. This requires humility and the ability to admit where you may have been wrong. Asking for forgiveness is a powerful way to show the other person you are committed to healing the relationship. Colossians 3:13 encourages us to forgive one another as God has forgiven us: "Bear with each other and forgive one another if any of you has a grievance against someone. Forgive as the Lord forgave you." Forgiveness is not just for the other person; it is also a gift to ourselves, freeing us from the heavy burden of resentment.

Rebuild Trust: In many broken relationships, trust has been damaged. Whether it was a betrayal, dishonesty, or failure to meet expectations, losing trust can create a barrier to healing. Rebuilding trust requires time, effort, and consistency. Trust is not restored overnight; it is rebuilt through actions that demonstrate reliability and commitment. This may involve being transparent in your actions, keeping promises, and showing that you can be depended upon. Each small step toward trustworthiness helps to repair the emotional bond that has been broken. It's important to understand that rebuilding trust is a gradual process. Patience and perseverance are necessary, as both parties may have doubts or fears about being hurt again. Through consistent behavior, the goal is to show that the relationship can once again be trusted. Proverbs 3:3-4 speaks to the importance of trustworthiness: "Let love and faithfulness never leave you; bind them around your neck, write them on the tablet of your heart. Then you will win favor and a good name in the sight of God and man." By committing to faithful and trustworthy behavior, we can restore trust in our relationships.

Set Boundaries: Sometimes, the healing process requires setting healthy boundaries. Boundaries help ensure that both parties feel respected and valued in the relationship. They also help prevent future hurt by establishing clear expectations for behavior. Boundaries are not meant to create distance but to protect the relationship from further damage. They allow both individuals to express what they are comfortable with and what they are not. For example, you may need to set boundaries around handling disagreements, ensuring that both parties remain respectful and refrain from hurtful words. Communicate these boundaries clearly and kindly. Boundaries should be mutually agreed upon and understood as a tool for maintaining a safe and healthy relationship. Healthy boundaries allow for the space needed for both emotional and relational healing. Galatians 6:2 reminds us to "Carry each other's burdens, and in this way, you will fulfill the law of Christ." This can include respecting each other's limits and boundaries to foster a more loving and caring relationship.

Focus on the Positive: While the focus of healing is often on resolving conflicts and addressing hurt, it's equally important to remember the positive aspects of the relationship. What brought you together in the first place? What are the strengths of the relationship? Reflecting on the good times and shared experiences can reignite feelings of love, appreciation, and connection. By focusing on the positive, you can shift the relationship dynamic away from conflict and toward growth and renewal. Celebrate the small victories as the relationship heals, and take time to appreciate both parties' efforts. Gratitude can be a powerful tool in mending a broken relationship. Philippians 4:8 encourages us to dwell on what is good: "Finally, brothers and sisters, whatever is true, whatever is noble, whatever is right, whatever is pure, whatever is lovely, whatever is admirable—if anything is excellent or praiseworthy—think about such things." Focusing on the positive can create an atmosphere of hope and healing.

The Joy of Reconciliation

Reconciliation is more than conflict resolution; it is a powerful opportunity for new beginnings. When relationships are healed, they often come out stronger and more resilient. The process of reconciliation is a journey that involves forgiveness, understanding, and love. When that journey leads to a place of restored connection, it marks the start of a fresh chapter in the relationship, filled with renewed hope and potential. Embracing new beginnings after reconciliation means celebrating the progress that has been made. Recognizing the growth that has occurred through the trials and conflicts that once divided the relationship is essential. Each step of the healing process, from acknowledging the problem to offering forgiveness, has contributed to the strength and resilience of the relationship. These challenges have built a foundation of trust and understanding, allowing the relationship to emerge stronger than before.

The Bible offers many examples of reconciliation leading to new beginnings. One powerful example is the story of Jacob and Esau in Genesis 33. After years of conflict and estrangement, Jacob and Esau reconciled, leading to a heartfelt reunion and a restored relationship. This story reminds us that, with God's help, even the most broken relationships can be mended and renewed. In relationships, healing can transform past wounds into stepping stones toward a deeper connection. After going through a season of difficulty, you can rebuild the relationship with a greater appreciation for one another. Reconciliation strengthens the emotional bonds between individuals, creating a deeper understanding of each other's needs, feelings, and perspectives. As you enter this new beginning, take time to celebrate the progress that has been made. Healing broken relationships takes time, effort, and patience, and reaching a place of peace and understanding is an achievement worth acknowledging. This celebration can be a simple expression of gratitude for one another, an affirmation of both parties' hard work in the healing process, or a shared experience that brings joy to the relationship. Celebrating progress does not mean that all problems are entirely behind you. Healing is ongoing, but recognizing milestones helps solidify the positive changes. It also fosters an atmosphere of appreciation and respect, encouraging both parties to continue investing in the relationship. Romans 12:10: "Be devoted to one another in love. Honor one another above yourselves." As you celebrate the progress in your relationship, take this time to honor the efforts you and the other person have made to restore your connection. Mutual appreciation and gratitude will help strengthen the bond as you move forward.

Reconciliation allows for a renewed connection that is often richer and deeper than before. The process of healing broken relationships enables both parties to reflect on the value of their bond and the importance of maintaining it. As a result, there is a greater appreciation for one another and a renewed sense of commitment to keeping the relationship strong. This new beginning is a time to embrace the positive changes from healing. It may involve redefining certain aspects of the relationship or setting new expectations for how you will communicate, resolve conflicts, and support one another. This renewed connection brings the possibility of more meaningful interactions, a stronger sense of trust, and a deeper level of mutual respect. Proverbs 27:9, "Perfume and incense bring joy to the heart, and the pleasantness of a friend springs from their heartfelt advice." Embracing the renewed connection allows for deeper intimacy and heartfelt conversations that bring great joy and fulfillment to both parties. As you move forward in your healing journey, consider the impact your story can have on others. Reconciliation and healing are not just personal victories; they can be powerful testimonies that inspire and encourage others facing similar struggles. Sharing your journey of healing and forgiveness can help others see that restoration is possible and that broken relationships can be mended. By sharing your story, you invite others into your vulnerability. Being open about your challenges hurts, and the reconciliation process can give others the courage to confront their relational struggles. Vulnerability creates a space for empathy and understanding, allowing people to connect with your experience more deeply. Sharing your journey doesn't mean revealing every detail or revisiting all the pain, but offering insights into the healing process can be incredibly impactful. Your story may give someone the hope to pursue reconciliation in their relationship. It can also encourage others to believe in the power of forgiveness and the possibility of starting anew. 2 Corinthians 1:4, "[God] comforts us in all our troubles so that we can comfort those in any trouble with the comfort we receive from God." The comfort you have found in your healing journey can be a source of strength and encouragement for others.

Inspiring others through your story can create healing and reconciliation in families, communities, and beyond. When people see the power of forgiveness and the renewal of relationships, they are often moved to reflect on their relationships and consider making efforts to heal. Sharing can lead to conversations about forgiveness, empathy, and restoration. You may find that your journey encourages others to seek healing in their relationships or helps prevent future conflicts from escalating. You can contribute to a broader culture of forgiveness and understanding by modeling reconciliation and the joy from renewed relationships. Hebrews 10:24-25 urges us to encourage and spur each other toward love and good deeds. Your healing and reconciliation story can inspire someone else to take the first step toward mending a broken relationship. It's important to remember that healing is an ongoing process. While reconciliation may mark the beginning of a new chapter, relationships require continuous effort to thrive. Healing doesn't stop after forgiveness is offered and trust is rebuilt; it requires ongoing communication, love, and understanding to maintain the renewed connection. Keeping the lines of communication open is essential for sustaining a healthy relationship. Continue to engage in open and honest conversations with the other person, ensuring that any future concerns or misunderstandings are addressed quickly and kindly. Make it a priority to check in with one another, share your thoughts and feelings, and listen attentively to the other person's perspective. Regular communication helps to prevent minor issues from escalating and ensures that both parties feel heard and valued. As you progress in your healed relationship, consciously prioritize love and understanding in all your interactions. Be patient with one another, and approach each challenge with grace and empathy. Love is the foundation of any strong relationship, and showing love through your actions, words, and attitudes will help the relationship flourish. Ephesians 4:2: "Be completely humble and gentle; be patient, bearing with one another in love." By choosing to respond with love and understanding, you can nurture the relationship and ensure it continues to grow. Even after reconciliation, it's important to remember that forgiveness and grace are ongoing. No relationship is perfect; there may be moments when hurtful words or actions occur again. When these moments arise, forgive quickly and extend grace to the other person. By cultivating a spirit of forgiveness, you create an environment where love and respect can thrive, even in difficult moments. Continuing to forgive when needed will keep the relationship strong and prevent unresolved issues from creating distance.

CHAPTER 6

EQUIPPING THE FAMILY FOR SPIRITUAL WARFARE

The family is designed to be a solid spiritual unit. When each member is spiritually equipped, the family can stand together against the enemy's attacks. Families can face challenges such as temptation, division, and conflict; understanding the spiritual warfare influencing these challenges is crucial. It's essential to realize that our enemies are not one another but the spiritual forces trying to disrupt our unity and faith. By recognizing the true enemy, families can work together to combat these influences and support one another. Start by instilling biblical principles in your family. Regularly read and discuss the Bible, focusing on verses highlighting the importance of faith, prayer, and God's promises. Teach your children how these principles apply to their lives and how they can be used in spiritual warfare. As parents or guardians, it's essential to model a strong faith in action. Show your family what it means to rely on God during difficult times, and share personal testimonies of how faith has helped you overcome challenges. Children learn by example, so demonstrating your faith practically will encourage them to do the same.

Establish a regular family prayer time where everyone can come together to pray. This could be during meals, before bedtime, or a dedicated time during the week. Encourage everyone to share their prayer requests and pray for each other's needs. This practice strengthens family bonds and creates a supportive environment. Help children understand the importance of prayer by teaching them how to pray. Explain that prayer is a conversation with God, where they can express their thoughts, feelings, and requests. Encourage them to pray for others, their friends, and even for guidance in their daily lives. Encourage family members to memorize key Bible verses related to spiritual warfare, such as Ephesians 6:10-18 (the Armor of God) and James 4:7 (resisting the devil). Memorizing Scripture equips the family to use God's Word as a weapon against the enemy's lies and attacks. Share and discuss stories from the Bible that illustrate spiritual battles and victories, such as David and Goliath (1 Samuel 17) or the temptation of Jesus (Matthew 4:1-11). These stories can inspire and encourage family members to trust in God's power during their battles.

Encourage family members to build strong relationships with one another. Spend quality time together, engage in fun activities, and support each other's interests. Strong relationships create a supportive network where everyone feels safe to share their struggles and seek help. Teach the importance of forgiveness within the family. When conflicts arise, encourage open communication and a willingness to forgive. Holding onto grudges can create division, while forgiveness promotes healing and unity. Incorporate worship into your family life. This can be through singing, listening to worship music, or participating in church activities together. Worship creates an atmosphere of reverence and connection to God, strengthening the family's spiritual foundation. Encourage your family to participate in church activities, such as attending services, joining small groups, and serving in ministry. Being involved in a church community helps families grow spiritually and provides additional support during spiritual battles. Form relationships with other families who share similar values and beliefs. This can create a support network where families can pray for one another and share experiences in facing spiritual challenges. Teach your family to rely on the Holy Spirit for guidance and strength in spiritual warfare. Encourage them to be sensitive to the Holy Spirit's promptings and to seek His wisdom in their decisions. Help family members discover and develop their spiritual gifts. Understanding their gifts can empower them to contribute to the family and community, using their strengths in spiritual battles.

Leading Your Family with Faith

Leading a family is a significant responsibility, especially for those who desire to honor God in their homes. Leadership means guiding, nurturing, and providing for your loved ones. It involves making decisions that reflect God's love and wisdom. A leader is not just someone who gives orders but someone who serves and protects their family. Jesus is the ultimate example of a leader. He demonstrated servant leadership, putting others' needs above His own. As you lead your family, strive to follow Christ's example by being humble, compassionate, and supportive. As a leader, prioritize your family's spiritual growth. Encourage regular Bible reading, prayer, and discussions about faith. Create an environment where spiritual matters are openly discussed and everyone feels comfortable sharing their thoughts and questions. Your actions speak louder than words. Show your family what it means to live a life of faith by demonstrating integrity, honesty, and love in your daily interactions. Your example will inspire them to develop their relationship with God. Make prayer a central part of your family life. Set aside time each day to pray together. This could be during meals, before bed, or at a specific time that works for everyone. Use this time to lift each other's needs, express gratitude, and seek God's guidance. Teach family members the importance of personal prayer. Encourage them to talk to God about their thoughts, fears, and desires. Help them understand that prayer is a powerful tool in building their faith and combating spiritual challenges.

Foster an atmosphere of open communication where family members feel safe sharing their feelings and concerns. Encourage honesty and transparency, clarifying that everyone's voice matters in the family. Demonstrate unconditional love and acceptance. Remind your family that they are valued and cherished. When they feel secure in your love, they are more likely to thrive spiritually and emotionally. Involve your family in seeking God's will for decisions that affect everyone. Pray together for guidance and listen to the Holy Spirit's leading. Encourage family members to share their insights and ideas, fostering a sense of teamwork. Sometimes, the path ahead may be unclear. Remind your family to trust God's plan, even when circumstances are challenging. Encourage them to lean on God's promises and stay hopeful in uncertainty.

When challenges arise, tackle them as a family. Discuss the issues openly and pray for wisdom and strength. Encourage one another to remain steadfast in faith and to seek solutions together. Conflict is a natural part of family life. Teach the importance of forgiveness and reconciliation. Encourage family members to address grievances openly and seek to restore relationships. This practice fosters healing and unity. Ensure that your family understands the core values of Christianity, such as love, kindness, honesty, and respect. Use everyday situations as teaching moments to reinforce these values and explain how they align with Scripture. Encourage your family to serve others, whether through volunteering or helping neighbors. Service helps instill a sense of compassion and reminds them of the importance of loving others as Christ loves us. During difficult times, demonstrate calmness and trust in God. Your ability to stay focused on faith will reassure your family and help them navigate challenges with a clear mind. Remind your family that seeking help and relying on God's strength is okay. Share your experiences relying on God during tough times, illustrating how faith can carry us through adversity.

Establishing a Praying Household

Creating a praying household is essential for fostering a solid spiritual foundation within your family. Prayer is a way to communicate with God and a powerful tool for building unity, peace, and support among family members. Prayer allows your family to connect with God and create a personal relationship. It helps everyone understand His love, guidance, and promises. This connection strengthens your faith and encourages spiritual growth. Praying together fosters intimacy and unity among family members. It creates a safe space to share their thoughts, feelings, and concerns. This open communication leads to deeper relationships and a supportive environment. Prayer can bring comfort and clarity during difficult times. It reminds your family to rely on God's wisdom and strength, helping to alleviate fears and anxieties. This reliance on prayer cultivates peace within the household.

Establish a regular schedule for family prayer. This could be at meals, before bed, or during designated family time. Consistency is critical to making prayer a natural part of your family's routine. Designate a quiet area in your home for worship. This space should be comfortable and free from distractions. Having a specific place for prayer can help family members feel more focused and engaged during their time with God. Encourage your family to express gratitude during worship. Thanking God for His blessings fosters a spirit of appreciation and helps everyone recognize the good things in their lives. Teach your family to pray for others, whether friends, family, or those in need. Interceding for others strengthens your family's bond and cultivates compassion and empathy. Encourage family members to bring their requests before God. This includes personal needs, challenges, and dreams. This practice reinforces the idea that God cares about every aspect of their lives.

Encourage each family member to set aside time for personal prayer. This individual connection with God is essential for spiritual growth. Support them in finding a routine that works for them in the morning or at night. Create opportunities for family members to share their individual prayer experiences. This could be during family meetings or designated sharing times. Sharing helps everyone see how God answers prayers and reinforces the power of personal prayer. Incorporate Bible verses into your family's prayers. Reading Scripture before praying can guide your thoughts and help you focus on God's promises. You can take turns choosing verses that resonate with everyone. Encourage family members to memorize key Bible verses about prayer and faith. This practice can provide comfort and encouragement during times of need, reminding everyone of God's presence.

Make it a tradition to pray during family gatherings and special occasions. Whether it's holidays, birthdays, or family reunions, inviting God's presence into these moments can strengthen the bond within the family. When facing difficulties, come together as a family to pray for guidance and strength. This collective prayer can help everyone feel supported and encouraged during tough times. Encourage family members to keep a prayer journal where they can write down prayer requests and answers to prayers. This journal serves as a reminder of God's faithfulness and helps everyone see. Teach children that worship doesn't have to be complicated. Encourage them to talk to God as they would to a friend. Use simple language and relatable examples to help them understand the importance of prayer. Involve children in the family prayer time. Encourage them to pray out loud, share their thoughts, or suggest topics for prayer. This participation helps them feel valued and invested in the family's spiritual life.

Teaching Children to Identify and Resist Leviathan
Teaching children to identify and resist the Leviathan spirit is crucial for their spiritual growth and well-being. The Leviathan spirit can manifest in various ways, such as through pride,

division, and confusion. By equipping children with the tools to recognize these traits, you can help them develop a strong foundation of faith that empowers them to stand firm against negative influences. Start by explaining the Leviathan spirit in simple terms. You might say it represents things that make us feel proud, confused, or argumentative. Use relatable examples, such as feeling superior to others or causing disagreements among friends. Children often learn best through stories. Share biblical stories or parables that illustrate the characteristics of the Leviathan spirit. For instance, you might recount the story of King Nebuchadnezzar (Daniel 4), who struggled with pride before being humbled by God.

Teach children to identify behaviors that indicate the presence of the Leviathan spirit. These can include Arguing or refusing to listen to others, feeling overly proud or boastful, ignoring the feelings of others, and focusing only on oneself. Discuss these behaviors openly and encourage children to share their experiences. Help children reflect on their actions. Ask questions like, "Have you ever felt like you were better than someone else?" or "How do you feel when you argue with a friend?" This self-awareness is critical to recognizing when the Leviathan spirit may influence their thoughts and actions. Teach children about the importance of humility through scriptures like Philippians 2:3, which encourages us to consider others better than ourselves. Share examples of humble figures in the Bible, such as Jesus, who modeled servant leadership. Help children understand the value of unity and cooperation. Teach them verses like Ephesians 4:3, which encourages us to maintain unity. Discuss practical ways they can promote harmony among their friends and family. Incorporate prayer into your daily routine. Teach children to pray for humility and the strength to resist pride and division. Encourage them to ask God for guidance in their relationships and decision-making. Help children cultivate a spirit of gratitude by encouraging them to thank God for their blessings and those in their lives. This practice can reduce pride and entitlement, reinforcing a mindset of appreciation and contentment.

Create a safe space for children to discuss their feelings and experiences. Encourage them to talk about times when they felt prideful or divisive, and guide them in finding biblical solutions to these challenges. As parents and caregivers, model the behavior you want to see in your children. Show humility, practice forgiveness, and promote unity in your family. Children learn best through observation, so your example will speak volumes. Encourage children to speak up when they notice the Leviathan spirit in themselves or others. This empowerment helps them feel confident in addressing negative behaviors and seeking help. Offer books, videos, or games that reinforce the values of humility, unity, and love. These resources can help children understand and resist the Leviathan spirit engagingly. Encourage your children to participate in church activities like youth groups or service projects. Being part of a community fosters a sense of belonging and helps children learn from others' examples of humility and service. Engage in volunteer work as a family. Assisting others teaches children the importance of putting others first and strengthens their resistance to selfishness and pride.

CHAPTER 7

THE
TRANSFORMATIVE
POWER OF GRACE

race is the free and undeserved love and favor of God. It is not something we earn through our actions or good deeds; instead, it is a gift God freely gives us. Ephesians 2:8-9 reminds us that we are saved by grace through faith, and this is not from ourselves; it is the gift of God. Grace reflects God's immense love for us. He knows our weaknesses, mistakes, and failures but loves us anyway. This love is not conditional on our performance but is given freely, allowing us to come to Him as we are. Grace has the power to heal wounds from our past. Many of us carry the weight of regret, guilt, or shame from our mistakes. When we accept God's grace, we can release these burdens and experience true healing. Romans 8:1 tells us that there is no condemnation for those in Christ Jesus, freeing us to move forward without the chains of our past holding us back. Grace transforms our identity. Instead of seeing ourselves through the lens of our failures, we begin to see ourselves as God sees us: beloved, forgiven, and made new. 2 Corinthians 5:17 states that if anyone is in Christ, they are a new creation; the old has passed away, and the new has come. This shift in perspective allows us to walk confidently in our new identity.

Grace empowers us to change and grow. While we may struggle with sin or destructive patterns in our lives, grace gives us the strength to overcome them. Titus 2:11-12 tells us that God's grace teaches us to say no to ungodliness and worldly passions and to live self-controlled, upright, and godly lives. Through grace, we find the power to live in a way that honors God. Embracing grace means living daily in awareness of God's love and forgiveness. This awareness shapes our thoughts, actions, and interactions with others. It encourages us to extend grace to ourselves and others, fostering a culture of forgiveness and understanding. When faced with difficulties, grace reminds us that we are not alone. God's grace is sufficient for us, even in our weakness (2 Corinthians 12:9). This assurance allows us to face challenges with courage and resilience, knowing that God is with us and supports us. Grace transforms our relationships. As we experience God's grace, we learn to extend that same grace to those around us. This creates an environment of love, acceptance, and forgiveness in our families, friendships, and communities. Ephesians 4:32 encourages us to be kind and compassionate to one another, forgiving each other, just as in Christ, God forgave us. We are called to be vessels of grace to others as we receive grace. This means sharing God's love and kindness with those around us. When we demonstrate grace, we reflect God's character, drawing others to Him. Recognizing the transformative power of grace leads to a life filled with gratitude. When we acknowledge the ways God has worked in our lives, we can't help but express our thankfulness. This gratitude fuels our worship and deepens our relationship with God.

Finding Strength in Grace

Grace is a powerful and life-altering gift from God. In 2 Corinthians 12:9, "But he said to me, 'My grace is sufficient for you, for my power is made perfect in weakness.' Therefore, I will boast all the more gladly about my weaknesses so that Christ's power may rest on me." The Apostle Paul is sharing his experience of struggling with a "thorn in the flesh." This thorn represents a persistent problem or challenge that caused him distress. Despite his prayers and pleas for relief, God chose not to remove it. Instead, God revealed a profound truth: His grace is enough. Paul's admission of weakness is essential. We often try to hide our weaknesses or view them as failures. However, recognizing our limitations is the first step toward finding strength in grace. God's grace shines brightest in our weakest moments.

The Sufficiency of Grace: "My grace is sufficient for you" comes from 2 Corinthians 12:9, where God reassures us that His grace is enough to meet all our needs. Grace is God's undeserved kindness and love, given freely to us. It doesn't mean our problems will go away, but it does mean that God will provide us with the strength and support we need to face them. When we feel weak, tired, or overwhelmed, God's grace gives us the strength to keep going. It helps us face life's challenges with courage and confidence, knowing we are not alone. We don't have to rely on our abilities or strength because God is with us, and His power becomes visible when we lean on His grace. Grace gives us what we need to endure hard times, and even when life feels too heavy, we can trust that God is holding us up with His grace.

Finding Strength in Our Weakness: Often, we see weakness as a problem or something to be ashamed of. But the apostle Paul encourages us to think differently about it. Instead of viewing our weakness as a setback, we can see it as an opportunity for God's power to work through us. When we admit that we can't do everything independently and ask for God's help, He steps in and shows His strength. This shift in perspective allows us to embrace our struggles rather than fight against them. God's strength is made perfect in our weakness because, in those moments, we rely entirely on Him. We stop trying to solve everything ourselves and let God's grace carry us through. This doesn't mean we won't face difficulties, but it does mean that God's grace will always be enough to help us endure them. When we accept that, we find peace and strength amid our struggles.

The Role of Faith: Trusting in God's grace takes faith. Hebrews 11:1 defines faith as "confidence in what we hope for and assurance about what we do not see." Faith means trusting God knows what is best for us, even when we don't understand our circumstances. Faith in God's grace allows us to rest, knowing He works in our lives, even when we face challenges. We might not see the whole picture or understand why we are going through hard times, but faith reminds us that God is in control and that His grace is sufficient.

Walking in grace requires daily dependence on God. The more time we spend with God, the more we understand and appreciate His grace's depth. This deepens our faith and helps us trust Him more, even in difficult situations.

Practical Steps to Embrace Grace: Ask God to show you where you need His grace. Pray for the ability to trust Him more, especially in your weaknesses. When you pray, ask for His strength to face whatever challenges come your way. Think about times when you've experienced God's strength and grace. Remember how He helped you during tough times, and let that memory strengthen your faith for the future. Focus on Bible verses that speak about God's grace and strength. One powerful verse is Isaiah 40:29, "He gives strength to the weary and increases the power of the weak." Verses like this can remind you of God's constant support in your life. Being part of a community of faith is essential. Surround yourself with other believers who can encourage you in your faith journey. Share your struggles with them, and let them pray for you. Sometimes, the prayers of others help us see God's grace more clearly. Take time to recognize where God's grace has been evident in your life. Keep a gratitude journal where you write down instances of God's faithfulness. This practice will remind you of His grace and how He strengthens you, especially in times of weakness.

Grace That Sustains in Difficult Times

Everyone goes through difficult times. These can come from personal struggles, health issues, loss, or overwhelming challenges. Feeling discouraged, tired, or even alone during these moments is natural. However, God's grace is what can carry us through. Grace is not just a concept or an idea—it's a powerful gift from God that helps us endure life's most brutal storms. Grace is God's unearned favor toward us. This means we receive God's blessings, love, and support, even though we don't deserve them. It is a vital part of who God is. His grace is freely given, and we don't have to do anything special to earn it. God's grace is always there for us, especially during difficult times. God's grace sustains us when life gets hard. It doesn't mean that all of our problems will disappear, but it does mean that God's grace gives us the strength to keep going. 2 Even when we feel weak, God's grace is more than enough to carry us through. When life gets overwhelming, we can trust that God's grace will hold us up. In those moments when we feel like we can't take another step, God's grace strengthens us.

During tough times, we often feel lonely or lost. But God's grace brings comfort. 2 Corinthians 1:3-4 calls God the "Father of compassion and the God of all comfort, who comforts us in all our troubles." His grace wraps around us like a blanket, reminding us that we are never truly alone. Even when things are hard, and we feel no one understands, God is always there with His grace, offering comfort and peace. This comfort doesn't always take away the pain but reassures us that God is walking with us through it. Difficult times can make us feel hopeless, but God's grace offers hope. Romans 15:13, "May the God of hope fill you with all joy and peace as you trust in him." Even when our situation seems dark, we can trust God's grace to fill our hearts with hope, joy, and peace. When we rely on God's grace, we don't have to be controlled by fear or doubt. God's grace fills us with hope, reminding us that brighter days are ahead and that we can trust Him to care for us. Sometimes, we feel like we can't go on when the burden feels too heavy. But God's grace gives us the strength to endure. Philippians 4:13, "I can do all this through him who gives me strength." When we feel like we've reached our limit, God's grace empowers us to keep moving forward, one step at a time. It's not about us trying to be strong by ourselves. God's grace gives us the courage and energy to face each day, knowing He is with us and will never leave us.

Life can be chaotic, especially during difficult times. We may feel anxious, worried, or stressed. But God's grace brings us peace. Philippians 4:7, "The peace of God, which transcends all understanding, will guard your hearts and your minds in Christ Jesus." This means that even when things are falling apart, God's grace gives us peace that doesn't make sense in the natural world.

This peace guards our hearts, protecting us from the chaos and turmoil of life. It allows us to rest in God's promises, knowing He is in control. Don't go through tough times alone. Share your burdens with trusted friends, family members, or church members. They can offer encouragement, support, and prayer, helping you feel less isolated in your struggles. During difficult times, focus on the things you are thankful for. Gratitude helps shift your perspective from what is wrong to what is right. It lets you see how God's grace works in your life. Keeping a gratitude journal can help remind you of God's faithfulness. Hard times often help us grow stronger and become better versions of ourselves. James 1:2-4 encourages us to "consider it pure joy" when we face trials because they produce perseverance and maturity in our faith. When we rely on God's grace, we grow spiritually and emotionally. When others see how you rely on God's grace during difficult times, it can inspire them to seek God's grace, too. Your faith and strength can be a powerful testimony to others, showing them that God's grace is natural and available to everyone.

Moving from Brokenness to Wholeness

Life can often lead us through difficult experiences that leave us feeling broken and hurt. Whether due to personal struggles, relationship issues, loss, or trauma, we may find ourselves grappling with feelings of despair and hopelessness. However, through God's grace, healing is possible. Brokenness is when we feel shattered, incomplete, emotionally, or spiritually damaged. It can manifest as sadness, anger, confusion, or a sense of unworthiness. Many people experience brokenness at some point due to circumstances beyond their control. The death of a loved one, the end of a relationship, or losing a job can leave us feeling shattered. Experiencing rejection from family, friends, or society can profoundly impact our self-worth and sense of belonging. Traumatic experiences can leave lasting scars, making it difficult to move forward. Our actions and decisions can lead to guilt and shame, contributing to our sense of brokenness.

The first step toward healing is recognizing and accepting your feelings. It's essential to allow yourself to grieve and process the pain. Ignoring or suppressing emotions can hinder the healing process. God desires to be our healer. In Psalm 147:3, "He heals the brokenhearted and binds up their wounds." Turn to God in prayer, inviting Him into your pain. Pour out your heart to Him and seek His comfort. Understand that God's grace is sufficient for our weaknesses. 2 Corinthians 12:9 reminds us, "My grace is sufficient for you, for my power is made perfect in weakness." His grace empowers us to move from brokenness to wholeness, reminding us that we are loved and accepted despite our flaws. Often, we carry guilt and shame from past mistakes. Forgiving yourself is crucial for moving forward. Recognize that God has already forgiven you, and let go of the weight of regret. Romans 8:1, "Therefore, there is no condemnation for those in Christ Jesus." Holding onto bitterness and resentment only prolongs our suffering. Ephesians 4:32 encourages us to "be kind and compassionate to one another, forgiving each other, just as in Christ God forgave you." Forgiveness is a decisive step toward healing, allowing us to release the hurt and embrace freedom. Our identity in Christ is rooted in His love and acceptance. 2

Corinthians 5:17 declares, "Therefore, if anyone is in Christ, the new creation has come: The old has gone, the new is here!" Embrace your new identity as a beloved child of God, created with purpose and worth. As you move toward wholeness, allow God to redefine your life. Pursue passions and interests that bring you joy. Set new goals and step into His plans, trusting He guides your path.

CHAPTER 8

LIVING VICTORIOUSLY BEYOND LEVIATHAN

As a believer in Christ, you are called to live in victory. Romans 8:37 tells us, "No, in all these things, we are more than conquerors through him who loved us." Recognizing your identity as a conqueror equips you to face challenges with confidence. Jesus has all authority in heaven and on earth (Matthew 28:18), and this authority is given to you as a believer. You can resist the Leviathan spirit and declare your victory over it. Ephesians 6:16 reminds us to take up the shield of faith, which can extinguish all the flaming arrows of the evil one. A strong faith in God's promises will protect you from the attacks of the Leviathan spirit. Strengthening your faith involves spending time in God's Word, prayer, and worship. The more you immerse yourself in His presence, the more your faith will grow, allowing you to stand firm against adversity. God's promises are powerful tools in your spiritual arsenal. To live victoriously, you must actively resist the influence of the Leviathan spirit. This involves recognizing its signs and taking a stand against it through prayer and spiritual warfare. Understanding and embracing your God-given purpose is vital for living victoriously. Ephesians 2:10 reminds us that we are God's handiwork, created for good works. Engage in activities that align with your calling and bring you joy. Living beyond the Leviathan spirit also involves serving others. By focusing on helping those around you, you shift your perspective from self to service, fostering a sense of fulfillment and joy.

Embracing Your Identity in Christ

Understanding who you are in Christ is a powerful part of your faith journey. The Bible teaches us that accepting Jesus as your Savior makes you a new creation. This transformation is described in 2 Corinthians 5:17, which says, "If anyone is in Christ, they are a new creation. The old has passed away; behold, the new has come!" This means that your past mistakes, regrets, and failures no longer define you. Instead, your new identity as a child of God is what truly matters. Embracing your identity in Christ helps you break free from guilt, shame, and condemnation. Instead of seeing yourself as someone unworthy or flawed, you can understand that you are loved and accepted by God. 1 John 3:1 reminds us of this incredible truth: "See what great love the Father has lavished on us, that we should be called children of God!" This unique relationship with God shows that you have great value and worth simply because He loves you. As a believer, you also have authority over spiritual forces that may try to harm you or lead you astray. In Luke 10:19, Jesus says, "I have given you authority to trample on snakes and scorpions and to overcome all the power of the enemy." This authority comes not from your own strength but from the victory that Christ won over sin and death. Knowing this helps you stand firm against challenges and obstacles. In Ephesians 6:11-13, we are encouraged to put on the whole armor of God so that we can stand against the devil's schemes. Recognizing that you are equipped for battle against negative influences, such as the Leviathan spirit, strengthens your resolve and helps you resist temptation.

Embracing your identity in Christ means living out your faith every day. Galatians 2:20 says, "I have been crucified with Christ, and I no longer live, but Christ lives in me." This means you don't face life alone. Jesus is with you, helping you through every struggle and challenge. Knowing that Christ lives in you empowers you to walk with confidence and courage. As you embrace this identity, you are also called to reflect Christ's love in your relationships. 1 John 4:19 says, "We love because He first loved us." This love transforms how you treat others and helps you overcome feelings of isolation or conflict that may arise from negative influences. Embracing your identity in Christ means acknowledging that you are not perfect and that it is okay to be weak at times. 2 Corinthians 12:9 reminds us, "My grace is sufficient for you, for my power is made perfect in weakness." When you lean on Christ's strength instead of relying on your own, you can overcome the challenges of negative influences. Recognizing your weaknesses allows you to receive God's grace and power. As a believer, you have the Holy Spirit living inside you. John 14:26 says, "The Holy Spirit will teach you all things and remind you of everything I have said to you." This means that the Holy Spirit is your helper, guiding you in truth and helping you resist temptation. When you rely on the Holy Spirit, you can live according to your true identity in Christ. One effective way to embrace your identity is by speaking God's truth over your life. Use affirmations based on Scripture to remind yourself of who you are in Christ. Say things like: "I am a child of God." "I am more than a conqueror." "I am loved and valued." These declarations reinforce your identity and help combat negative thoughts or feelings that may come your way.

Creating a Legacy of Faith

Creating a legacy of faith means building a foundation that can influence future generations. This legacy is about sharing your beliefs, values, and experiences with your family and community. It helps others understand God's goodness and encourages them to develop their faith. Psalm 78:4 tells us to share the great things God has done. This is important because it helps the next generation see how faithful and powerful God is. Talking about your faith journey—how you've seen God work in your life— allows others understand who God is. Sharing stories of His love and support can also encourage your family to trust Him. Your actions often speak louder than your words. Hebrews 12:1 encourages us to run with perseverance the race marked out for us, surrounded by a great cloud of witnesses. When you live out your faith, you show others how to do the same. Your perseverance and trust in God can inspire your family to grow in their relationship with Him. It is essential to teach your family about the Bible and its teachings. Deuteronomy 6:6-7 tells us to impress God's commands on our children. You discuss biblical principles during everyday moments—like at breakfast or while driving and encouraging questions about faith and exploring the answers together. Creating an environment where everyone feels comfortable asking questions leads to deeper understanding and personal growth in their relationship with God. Participating in community service projects as a family is another excellent way to create a legacy of faith. Helping those in need shows Christ's love in action. It teaches your family valuable lessons about compassion, kindness, and serving others. Faith is not just about what you believe but also about what you do. Teach your family the value of prayer to talk to God. Encourage them to share their thoughts, feelings, and needs with Him. This practice helps them build a closer relationship with God, as a parent, model personal devotion by setting aside time for prayer and Bible study. Let your family see you engage with God's Word and pray. This shows that faith is a personal journey that requires commitment and effort. Regularly pray for your family members, asking God to help them grow in their faith. James 5:16 reminds us that the prayer of a righteous person is powerful and effective. Your prayers can profoundly impact their spiritual journeys, drawing them closer to God. Take time to bless your children and future generations with your words. Speak encouragement and affirm their identity in Christ. Remind them of God's promises for their lives. This fosters hope and strengthens their faith in the future.

Walking in Freedom and Purpose

True freedom is more than just being free from rules or limits. It means living fully in the way God wants you to live. When you walk in this freedom, you can fulfill your purpose and live a life that brings glory to God. Galatians 5:1, "It is for freedom that Christ has set us free. Stand firm, then, and do not let yourselves be burdened again by a yoke of slavery." Jesus has freed us from the chains of sin and guilt. When we accept Christ as our Savior, we break free from the destructive patterns that once held us back. Sin can trap us, making us feel like we can never change or do better. But through Jesus, we can overcome these struggles. Romans 6:22, "But now that you have been set free from sin and have become slaves of God, the benefit you reap leads to holiness, and the result is eternal life." This means that you gain a new life filled with purpose when you follow Christ. You become part of God's family and start to live in a way that honors Him. Every person has a particular purpose that God has planned just for them. Ephesians 2:10, "For we are God's handiwork, created in Christ Jesus to do good works, which God prepared in advance for us to do." This means you are not here by accident. God created you with specific gifts and talents to make a difference. To find out your purpose, seek God through prayer, reading the Bible, and talking with other believers. They can help guide you and offer insight into the gifts you have. 1 Peter 4:10 encourages us to "use our gifts to serve others as faithful stewards of God's grace." Whether you are good at teaching, serving, promoting, or leading, use your talents to help others and glorify God.

It's essential to let go of past hurts, mistakes, and regrets to walk in freedom. Philippians 3:13-14 reminds us to forget what is behind and focus on what lies ahead. This means not letting your past define or hold you back from God's plan for your life. The Leviathan spirit often tries to deceive us with lies that can trap us in negative thinking. Identify any lies you have believed about yourself, like thinking you are not good enough or that you can't fulfill your purpose. Instead, embrace the truth of God's Word. Psalm 139:14, "I praise you because I am fearfully and wonderfully made." Remember that you are unique and loved by God. Seeking God's guidance as you walk in freedom and purpose is essential. Proverbs 3:5-6 encourages us to "trust in the Lord with all your heart and lean not on your understanding. In all your ways acknowledge Him, and He will make your paths straight." This means that we should rely on God to lead us and not just depend on our ideas. Set goals that align with God's purpose for your life. These goals might include growing personally, serving in your community, or helping others. Whatever your goals are, make sure they honor God and reflect your desire to serve. Walking in freedom and purpose does not mean there won't be challenges. Turning to God for strength and guidance is essential when tough times come. Isaiah 41:10 reminds us, "God is with us; we do not need to fear." He is our source of strength and will help us through our difficulties. Be aware of the Leviathan spirit, which can create division and confusion. Engage in prayer and spiritual warfare to fight against these negative influences. Remember that you have authority in Christ to overcome obstacles that stand in your way. As you walk in freedom and purpose, embrace the joy of knowing Christ. Nehemiah 8:10 says, "The joy of the Lord is our strength." Focusing on the good things in your life and the blessings from God will help you stay joyful. Let that joy overflow into everything you do. Walking in freedom and purpose also brings a profound sense of peace. Philippians 4:6-7 encourages us to present our requests to God and promises that His peace will guard our hearts and minds. Trusting in God's plan allows you to rest in His presence, knowing He is in control.

CONCLUSION

*Walking In Victory Over
The Leviathan Spirit*

O ne of the critical lessons in battling the Leviathan spirit is the power of humility. The Bible repeatedly teaches us that humility is one of the greatest weapons against pride, the main avenue through which this spirit works. In James 4:6, "God opposes the proud but shows favor to the humble." When we humble ourselves before God, we place ourselves under His protection, and the enemy's schemes lose power over us. Humility doesn't mean weakness or a lack of confidence. Instead, it means recognizing our need for God's help in every area of our lives. It means acknowledging that we can do nothing without Him, but we can overcome all things with Him. 1 Peter 5:6-7 "Humble yourselves, therefore, under God's mighty hand, that He may lift you in due time. Cast all your anxiety on Him because He cares for you." We must cultivate humility to walk in lasting victory over the Leviathan spirit. This involves regularly examining our motives, submitting our plans to God, and repenting when we recognize pride creeping in. When we walk humbly, we create an environment where the enemy has no foothold.

Another critical aspect of maintaining victory in spiritual warfare is the consistent practice of prayer and discernment. Prayer is not just a tool we use in moments of crisis; it is the lifeline that keeps us connected to God and sensitive to His voice. As we pray, we invite God to intervene in our situations and give us wisdom to navigate spiritual battles. Discernment is distinguishing between what is from God and what is from the enemy. The Leviathan spirit thrives on confusion and deception, making discernment an essential gift in spiritual warfare. We must ask God to sharpen our spiritual senses to recognize the enemy's tactics and stand firm against them. The Word of God is our greatest weapon in the fight against spiritual darkness. As we saw in the temptation of Jesus, He overcame Satan's lies by quoting Scripture. In the same way, we can defeat the Leviathan spirit by standing firm on the truth of God's Word. The Bible gives us the wisdom, power, and authority to resist the enemy. One of the critical strategies of the Leviathan spirit is twisting the truth to create confusion. It tries to make us doubt God's promises, question His goodness, and second-guess our decisions. But when we know the Word of God, we can stand confidently in the truth and refuse to be swayed by deception. Hebrews 4:12, "For the word of God is alive and active. Sharper than any double-edged sword, it penetrates even to dividing soul and spirit, joints and marrow; it judges the thoughts and attitudes of the heart." To walk in victory over the Leviathan spirit, we must continually feed our minds and hearts with God's Word, allowing it to shape our thinking and actions.

The Leviathan spirit's primary goal is to cause division. It seeks to separate friends, families, and churches through misunderstandings, offenses, and pride. As believers, one of our most effective defenses against this spirit is to pursue unity at all costs. Psalm 133:1 says, "How good and pleasant it is when God's people live together in unity!" Unity does not mean we will always agree on everything, but we choose to love, forgive, and honor one another despite our differences. The enemy cannot thrive without unity, love, and peace. When we prioritize relationships and work together in harmony, we create an atmosphere where God's presence dwells and the enemy's influence is broken. In your personal life, family, and church, prioritize pursuing peace and unity. When conflicts arise, seek resolution quickly through communication, forgiveness, and prayer. Don't allow pride or offense to create division. Remember that the Leviathan spirit thrives in environments of strife, so guard your heart and relationships against it. Through Christ's sacrifice, we have been given the authority to live in freedom from the enemy's power. John 8:36, "So if the Son sets you free, you will be free indeed." This freedom is not just from sin but from every attack and influence of the enemy, including the Leviathan spirit. Living in freedom means walking confidently in your identity as a child of God. Knowing that your Heavenly Father loves, values, and protects you. The enemy may try to convince you otherwise, but the truth is that you are already victorious in Christ. Colossians 2:15 declares, "Having disarmed the powers and authorities, He made a public spectacle of them, triumphing over them by the cross."

As you continue your faith journey, you must recognize that spiritual growth is lifelong. Like any relationship, your relationship with God requires consistent nurturing, attention, and devotion. The battles you face, like overcoming the Leviathan spirit, allow you to grow deeper in your walk with Christ. It is about achieving victory in one battle, continually maturing in your faith, and becoming more like Jesus daily. One of the best ways to ensure ongoing spiritual growth is to stay deeply rooted in God's Word. The Bible is not just a collection of stories or rules; it is living and active. It guides, transforms, and strengthens us in every area of life. Psalm 1:2-3 compares those who meditate on God's Word to a tree planted by water streams, producing fruit every season. This means that when you consistently immerse yourself in Scripture, you will grow strong spiritually and bear fruit, even in challenging times. Don't wait for a crisis to turn to God's Word—make it a daily habit. Let it renew your mind, shape your decisions, and give you wisdom for every situation. As you grow in your knowledge of the Bible, you'll find it easier to resist the enemy's schemes, including the Leviathan spirit, because you will have a strong foundation of truth. Prayer is a weapon in spiritual warfare and a means of building a deeper relationship with God. Through prayer, you communicate with your Heavenly Father, bringing your concerns, joys, struggles, and thanksgiving before Him. Prayer strengthens your faith and reminds you that you are never alone in any battle. Prayer is also a space where God will reveal more of Himself, guiding your decisions and helping you grow in discernment. The more you talk with God, the more you will recognize His voice, direction, and comfort in every aspect of your life.

Spiritual growth requires persistence. There will be moments when you feel like you are not making progress or when challenges seem overwhelming, but growth often happens in the seasons when we persevere through difficulties. Galatians 6:9 encourages us, "Let us not become weary in doing good, for at the proper time we will reap a harvest if we do not give up." Don't give up when you face setbacks or struggles. Every challenge is an opportunity to deepen your faith, strengthen your resolve, and draw closer to God. Keep pursuing Him, even when you don't see immediate results. Spiritual growth is often slow and steady, leading to lasting transformation. Growing spiritually means trusting God even when you don't fully understand what He is doing. The battles you face, like dealing with the Leviathan spirit, may not always make sense initially, but trust that God is in control. As you grow in faith, you learn to walk by faith, not by sight, trusting in God's character and promises even when circumstances seem difficult. 2 Corinthians 5:7: "We live by faith, not by sight." Spiritual growth often happens when we step out in faith, believing God's Word, even when our feelings or situations tell us otherwise. It's about developing the confidence to trust that God's plan is always good, even in spiritual warfare.

Now that you have gained a deeper understanding of the Leviathan spirit and the spiritual warfare we face, it is time to walk forward in victory. Each day is an opportunity to apply your learned principles, stand firm in your faith, and trust God's power to overcome. When you encounter moments of confusion, division, or pride, remember that these are enemy tactics, and you have the tools to resist. Through prayer, humility, reliance on God's Word, and a commitment to unity, you can defeat the Leviathan spirit and live in the freedom that Christ has provided. As you move forward, keep these critical truths in mind:

- You are not alone in this battle—God is with you and fights for you.
- You have authority in Christ—use the power of His name to rebuke the enemy.
- You are called to walk in victory—trust God's promises and stand firm in your faith.

May you continue to grow in your understanding of spiritual warfare, walk in the victory Christ has given you, and live in the freedom and peace that comes from being a child of God. Remember, the battle belongs to the Lord; you are more than a conqueror through Him.

A SPECIAL CALL TO SALVATION & NEW BEGINNINGS FROM APOSTLE DR. DAVID PHILEMON

Dear Beloved,
God loves you deeply and has brought you to this moment for a reason. No matter your past, His love and forgiveness are available to you.

The Bible says in John 3:16, "For God so loved the world that He gave His one and only Son, that whoever believes in Him shall not perish but have eternal life." Jesus Christ came to save you, offering you a new life of purpose and peace.

If you're ready to accept Jesus as your Lord and Savior, pray this simple prayer:

The Salvation Prayer

"Heavenly Father, I come to You in the Name of Jesus. I acknowledge that I am a sinner in need of a Savior. I believe that Jesus Christ is Your Son, that He died for my sins, and that You raised Him from the dead. I repent of my sins and turn to You with my

Whole heart. Jesus, I ask You to come into my life. Be my Lord and my Savior. I surrender my life to You. Fill me with Your Holy Spirit, guide me on the path of righteousness, and help me to follow Your script for my life. Thank you, Father, for saving me. In the name of Jesus. Amen."

Welcome to the Family of God!

If you have just prayed this prayer, Congratulations! You are now a child of God, and heaven is rejoicing. Your journey has begun, and we're here to support you as you grow in faith and discover God's unique plans for you.

Next Steps:
• Connect with a Bible-believing church.
• Read the Bible Daily: God's Word is your guide.
• Pray Regularly: Prayer is your lifeline to God.
• Share Your Faith: Don't keep the good news to yourself.

www.ingramcontent.com/pod-product-compliance
Lightning Source LLC
Chambersburg PA
CBHW071904020426
42331CB00010B/2656